10

STRICTLY PERSONAL

Some Memoirs of Cecil H. King

STRICTLY PERSONAL

Some Memoirs of
CECIL H. KING

Weidenfeld and Nicolson
5 Winsley Street London W1

SBN 297 17772 9

Printed in Great Britain by
Cox & Wyman Ltd., London, Reading and Fakenham

Contents

Illustrations

Part One

Part One

My Early Years

I was born on 20 February 1901 at Poynters Hall, Totteridge, an eighteenth-century house of no distinction, now pulled down. My mother and father were on leave from India, and I was born in my grandmother Harmsworth's house. All my six brothers and sisters were born abroad, four in what is now Pakistan, two in Simla. At the time of my birth my mother was thirty-five and my father ten years older. After my birth the family returned to Simla, where the twins were born. My mother came home for good in 1903 and my father retired in 1905.

But perhaps I should go back in history. My great-great-grandfather was a bookseller and publisher in Dublin. He married Elizabeth Jane Hicks, daughter of a Dublin brewer. She was born in 1770, married in 1790 and died in 1838. He became a freeman of the city of Dublin in 1802, but he became involved with the Irish rebels of the day, lost his business, and died in poverty about 1820. His second son was my great-grandfather. He was born in 1797 and christened Luke White after his father's great friend Luke White, who was a very successful Irish publisher and bookseller and who became MP for Leitrim and father of the first Lord Annaly.

Luke White King entered Trinity College Dublin in 1817 and graduated with classical honours in 1822. He supported himself and his youngest brother for most of this time by coaching. He was ordained, became second master at Drogheda School in 1827 and headmaster from 1828 to 1832. When I was in

Drogheda some years ago I went to the school, which is still in existence, while Ennis College, County Clare, of which my great-grandfather was headmaster from 1832 to 1859, became a Catholic girls' school in the nineties, and is still continuing in what is mostly the old buildings.

Luke White King married his first wife in Drogheda in 1827. She was a Miss Ashe, daughter of a Protestant parson in Armagh. She died in 1840, aged thirty-four, of scarlet fever caught when nursing the boys at Ennis. She was described as 'tall and stately, with sharp features and large brown eyes, clever, conscientious and unaffected'. She had six children, of whom four survived her – Henry, my grandfather (1830–97), Lucas, grandfather of Francis King the author, George and Richard (1839–1930), who was my godfather.

Luke White's second wife was a cousin, Hannah Christie, who proved a harsh stepmother. Hannah's mother, with seven daughters on her hands, addressed them shortly after the death of the first Mrs King and said that if any one of them would like to be the second Mrs King, she should come with her on a visit to the widower. Hannah volunteered, and my great-grandfather seems to have fallen an immediate victim, as they were married at Booterstown, near Dublin, in 1841. She bore him three sons and a daughter. They were treated with special favour, sitting at the high table in the school hall and allowed toast, whereas her stepsons had meals with the other boys and no toast! The two elder boys went off to India, leaving George and Dick to face the ferocious temper of their father, the brutality of the school and the partiality of their stepmother.

Luke White married a third time in 1869, his second wife having died in 1861. The third time he was seventy-two and she was twenty-three! My father remembered visiting his grandfather after the latter's retirement to Enniskerry, and described him as a small, ugly, burly man, with a red pock-marked face, very blue eyes and white hair. I inherited his very nice silver tea service, which I have given to my son Michael. I seem to remember the date is 1823, in which case it is unlikely to have been originally his, as such a tea-set would have been beyond his means as early as 1823.

My grandfather, Henry King, was born in 1830 in the First Master's house in Drogheda Grammar School. He entered Trinity College Dublin in 1847, and was elected Scholar in 1850. He gained first-class honours in classics and logic and a gold medal in logic, among many other prizes. He then studied medicine, passing the Indian Medical Service examination in 1855.

Meanwhile he had met his cousin, Sophie Eccleston, when she was on a long visit to her grandmother Christie at Bray, County Wicklow. Her home was in New York – she was born either there or in Rochester, New York, in 1828. Her father, Edward Eccleston, had emigrated from Ireland and set up business importing Irish linen. California University has published the diary of Sophie's brother, Robert Eccleston, written in 1849 when he was nineteen, and vividly describing his hazardous journey with an older brother and others by ship from New York to Galveston to Port Lavaca, Texas, and then overland by covered wagon to California, where their descendants now live in Oakland. He failed to find any gold, but another cousin, one Anderson, made money selling water to the miners, and his descendant, when I met him, was the leading gynaecologist in San Francisco. The Oakland Ecclestons had letters, of which I took copies, from my great-grandmother Mary (*née* Christie) to her husband Edward Eccleston in New York (1823–6 and 1834–5). She was staying, with some of her children, with her mother in Ireland in order to save money.

In one of her letters to her husband, dated Bray (Co. Wicklow), 29 September 1824, Mary writes:

'You will warmly sympathize, I am sure, when I tell you the losses your friend Miss Corbett has sustained and the fright occasioned her a few nights ago after she had been asleep for some time. She was roused by hearing a noise at her room door and immediately concluded it must be the dog that had got into the house. At the same moment she heard a person breathing, and again concluded it was the servant man in search of him. But she was soon unhappily undeceived, for presently two soft hands came over her in the bed and a voice said, "Don't be alarmed, I will not harm you. I am a Robber come to plunder you of all your plate, watch and whatever money you have got in the house." He then tied her fast in the bed and covered her face with the sheet (this was all done in the dark). I should tell you there were three or four of them in the house beside and they took care to secure the servants likewise. After completing all this a light was produced and they commenced examining her drawers, et cetera. She had been in town a few days previous and brought out money to pay Mama the rent. However, they succeeded in taking all. Strong suspicion rests upon a servant man whom she had for some time and parted with lately, whom it was thought well acquainted with every turn of the house. The person who tied her was extremely polite for he suggested she should take a little wine or water before he took his leave. He brought her a glass of water but had not compassion enough to release her from her unpleasant situation. One of the servants by seven in the morning had gnawed the rope across with her teeth.'

Bray, 21 October 1834, from the same to the same. The voyage from New York to Liverpool:

'We were very sick the first weeks we were out with the exception of baby. Poor little things I did not know what to do with them, such a time as I had of it. I often wished myself back in New York again and so did all the children. I wrote you a few hasty lines from Liverpool on our arrival. Indeed at the time I hardly knew what I was doing I was so harried. I believe I mentioned to you that Jane went back to New York when we were about five or six days out. One of our cabin passengers, a Mr Hall, who was crossing for his health thought he would return as he did not find himself getting better. And indeed I don't think he could have lived to get over, so the Captain spoke a brig bound for New York. I should have told you that I found Jane very little use to me in minding the children – and so I told her. She was quite put out at my speaking to her and said she wish'd she had not come. I told her I'd be just as well without her, and perhaps before long she might have an opportunity of returning. Sure enough in a day or two after, the opportunity offered, so I went up to her and told her that there was one of the gentlemen going back and she was then at liberty to return if she wished. She said if I liked she would go: I told her I did not care: let her do as she pleased. She still wanted to know if I wished her to go. I still said, do as she liked. I know what she was about. She thought I could not possibly do without her and I would coax her to stay. But she was quite mistaken. I knew I could get as capable as her in the steerage and if I had asked her to remain I'd have had a pretty time of it with her. As it was she was too saucy. The first drink she asked the steward for on board was a tumbler of champagne or Madeira and water, and thought he had a great deal of impudence to refuse her. She said she would call to you to pay what she owed, but I don't expect she will. I got a very nice Scotch woman out of the steerage to help mind the children, but she would not come further than Liverpool. I then had to take another woman to come up to Dublin with me, so you may think I'd a pretty time of it. The children would hardly let those strange women go near them. The stewardess was very attentive. Unfortunately we had two rather elderly sickly gentlemen on board, Captain Dean and a Mr Parker, who could not bear the children to make the least noise. I had to get very angry with them two or three times for being so very unreasonable. For God knows if I did not do everything in my power to keep them quiet, but except you'd tie them down and stop their mouths up, nothing short would satisfy them. I never met with such disagreeable men. They knew nothing of domestic life. The

7

children, considering they were sick and so on, were remarkably good. I used to feel so bad when they'd say anything about their noise, and I doing all I could to keep them still, I'd sit down and cry for hours.'

Dublin, 6 December 1834. From the same to the same:

'I must say, my dearest Edward, I cannot but feel hurt with you for not sending me some money before this. It was the last request I made of you when we parted and you promised me you would do so. I have said so much in my former letter about how I spent the money you gave me and all the little necessaries I had to buy that it would be now useless to repeat it. I shall merely tell you how I stand at the moment, and believe me most sincerely I cannot accuse myself of spending one shilling, since I left you, uselessly. I have been in every way particular as saving as I could but you know we have to live. I cannot support such a family on nothing: have to keep three servants: pay for washing besides so many little things for the house. I owe at this present time 13 pounds and have not a shilling in my purse. I requested of your father yesterday to take my watch and see what it would bring. He did so, went every place he thought would be the best and all they gave for it was about ten pounds. They say originally it cost a good deal but it would not be worth more to them. However, I told him if it will bring only 3 or 4 pounds it must go today. They tell me that there is not a bit of coal in the house and many other things wanting which must be got. If I have to sell every stitch of my clothes I will do so before I borrow any more money. I hoped to have been spared being under a compliment to anyone during my visit here. But oh how my pride is hurt.'

From the same to the same, Dublin, 13 December 1834.

'I cannot for the life of me imagine what you mean or how in the name of wonder you think we are to live – surely not

1902. Cecil King in his pram, with an Indian Bearer, at Summer Hill, Simla, the official residence of his father, afterwards Sir Lucas King, who was at this period responsible for the salt revenue of Northern India.

1903. The first steps. Cecil King in the garden at Simla, with his elder sister Enid, and the faithful Bearer. It was in this house that his younger brother and sister (twins) were born. This was during the period of Lord Curzon's Viceroyalty of India and he was godfather to the younger brother.

1904. Back in England, at Totteridge, where Cecil King was born. A nursery picnic, perhaps on the grass of Totteridge Common. In the picture from left to right are the twins, Cecil and Enid. The centre adult is Nanny Bennet, the centre of their lives at that period.

In the nursery donkey cart, outside the family home. Nora, the eldest of the family, and Enid are with Cecil in the back.

on Air. And then only reflect Sophia,* Edward, Robert idling away so much of their time for want of means to send them to school. The thought almost maddens me. I am now going on ten weeks in Ireland and do you possibly think that twenty pounds could keep us all this time? If I did not stay so long in Bray I don't know what I should have done. Oh, Edward, how could you have me so! Surely I do not merit such neglect. If only you'd see the way I spend my days crying and fretting you would really pity me. It cost me crossing from Liverpool to Dublin £6 7s. 6d. besides paying my nurse and stewardess on board. I feared your Father wanted money and gave him five pounds so you see how much I had left. You, I suppose, imagine it must only take as much to keep us as it did yourself when you were over, never thinking that I have such a family to provide for, obliged to keep three servants, pay for washing and many other things too numerous to mention. I have not bought one shillingworth of dress since I came over. I even had not money to purchase a ribbon for my old winter hat. Your poor Father is going about from place to place with my watch endeavouring to do the best with it. He hates so to throw it away but all he can get for it is a few pounds. They even object to giving anything for it: say they'd rather not have it at all. In the meantime he had to borrow five pounds for me – he pretended it was for his own use – to keep us from starving and to pay some taxes. That makes 18 pounds I owe and I shall never be at rest until I can pay it. How different I thought my visit would have been over here, instead of begging and borrowing like a common pauper. I feel so hurt and ashamed I can hardly raise my head.'

The same to the same, Bray, 13 January 1835:

'I have a request to make of you my dearest Edward which you must not refuse, 'tis to get your likeness taken for me so that I can always wear it next my heart. I want to have one

* My grandmother.

that looks like you at present. The one in George's place don't resemble you so much now 'tis too boyish looking. Dearest Edward do not refuse me: you must grant me this one little request. I know if I were near you I could soon coax you by throwing my arms round your neck and giving you a sweet kiss. How I long to hear if you think you can get over next summer. Try all you can to accomplish it. Every day I feel more and more at being separated from you. I blame myself very much for leaving you. Why did you let me? If I could only lay my head on your bosom once more and rest there, nothing in this world could tempt me to leave you.'

To return to my grandfather, Henry King. On a piece of paper still extant he noted:

'3rd October 1853. Sophie promised to visit me.'

And again,

'17th March 1854. I parted from Sophie leaving her on board the "Constitution" in the Mersey.'

Having qualified for the Indian Medical Service, my grandfather sailed immediately for New York, and they were married in Emmanuel Church on 3 September 1855.

After a short stay in Ireland, they embarked for India on 16 January 1856 and landed in Madras on 14 May. I remember my grandmother telling me that they went round the Cape and occupied a cabin which they had to furnish themselves. They had to do all their own washing on the return journey: with two small children they had to bring a cow, the only possible way of ensuring a supply of milk.

The year following their arrival in Madras, the Indian Mutiny broke out, and though there were no disturbances there, they had a notice chalked on the door of their house that they and their children (my father and his brother) would be thrown down the well, as had happened to English people in Cawnpore.

My grandfather spent much of his Service life in Madras and the rest in the Central Provinces. His work kept him following the troops on long marches on which my grandmother went with him. It was a hard life and she buried two, or perhaps three children in remote parts of India.

My grandfather died before I was born. He was short, with a long beard, and was surprised and hurt that he received less promotion than he thought he deserved. He seems to have been a good doctor. He wrote the standard book of the day on tropical hygiene, but he was a Fenian and refused to stand up when the band played 'God Save the Queen' at official functions. He also contributed lampoons on his superiors to the Madras newspapers under the pseudonym 'Josiah Paddlebox'.

Though my grandfather died in 1897, having retired as Deputy Surgeon-General on a pension of £900 a year in 1884, my grandmother lived on and died in Dublin in 1917 at the age of eighty-nine. She was a sweet old lady, always dressed in black, with a white cap on her head. There was no trace of her American origin, or of the very real hardships she must have endured in India.

My grandfather's youngest full brother was Richard Ashe King, Uncle Dick. As he only died in 1930, and was my godfather, I knew him well. Furthermore, it was his friendship with Kitty Maffett, my mother's cousin, that brought my father and mother together. When I knew Uncle Dick, he was a lively, witty old man, with a fund of funny stories. He began life as a parson, and in the middle of the last century was a curate in Cork. I have a manuscript biography he wrote – very dull stuff except for one story. He was leaving the Cork Hospital when he fell into step with the Catholic priest, who had also been visiting one of his parishioners. The priest was amused by something one of his flock had told him – it was not in confession, so could be repeated. The man who told the story evidently thought it edifying and suitable for a priest. The narrator had decided to shoot a local landlord (this was the period of agrarian outrages), and lay in wait for him on a lonely road – but his gun misfired. So he raced over the fields to get a second shot, but again the gun misfired. But the third time he said, 'In the name of the Father, and of the Son, and of the Holy Ghost' and pulled the trigger – and, 'Sure he dropped like a bird'.

Subsequently, Uncle Dick became curate to his uncle, Canon Burnett, at Bradford Parish Church (now Cathedral) and later, from 1867 to 1881, Vicar of Low Moor nearby. The stipend was a thousand a year, a large figure in those days. However, after a time he came to disbelieve the Anglican tenets, so he threw up his living (his only source of income) and cycled to London to earn a living by his pen. He was much loved at Bradford, and I remember being with him when a group of parishioners arrived to greet him on his birthday, fifty years after he had left the parish. I don't know quite what his literary work consisted of other than university extension lecturing and book reviewing. He published a number of books – a good life of Swift and of Goldsmith – under his own name, and a number of three-decker novels under the pseudonym 'Basil'. One of these latter was a very decorous job entitled *Passion's Slave*.

He was a keen cyclist at a time when cycling on what was called the 'safety bicycle' was quite new. He told me he could remember attending some cycle races where the runaway winners had fitted the first pneumatic tyres. This was in Dublin. I believe the original Dunlop was an Irish doctor. Anyway, the tyres had an inner tube which was protected by winding adhesive tape round both tyre and rim.

He used to get annoyed with my father, who was anxious to prove our relationship with the earls of Kingston. He was always asking Uncle Dick to recall evidence that would help him in his quest. Eventually, exasperated, Uncle Dick told the story of a *nouveau riche* peer who asked the College of Heralds to trace his ancestry. After some months' research, they announced they had traced his lordship's forebears to an actor who had played the part of the rear end of a donkey in a pantomime. The genealogical researches were then wound up! Actually the birth and marriage certificates of the place and period that might prove or disprove the point were burnt in a church fire early in the last century. We have, however, borne the same Kingston arms since John King's day.

Late in life, Uncle Dick married a sweet little woman, Maidie, sister of Field-Marshal Sir Claud Jacob, and aunt of General Sir Ian Jacob, former head of the BBC.

My father, Lucas White King, was born in Madras in 1856. His parents brought him back to Ireland and left him with his grand-uncle by marriage, the Rev. Robert Humphreys, afterwards Dean of Killaloe, in 1864. He was just eight. In his diary of that date, my grandfather wrote: 'When shall we see our dear little boy again, or whether we shall ever see him again, God only knows. We can only hope and pray. I feel that we have done our best for him in leaving him under Robert Humphreys' care. We shall do what more we can by sparing no expense on his education.'

My father's first schooling was at Tulla Rectory, County Clare, and in January 1870 he went on to Ennis College, in due course becoming a prefect and head of the school. He won many prizes and six silver medals in classics, French, English and for good conduct.

My father entered Trinity College Dublin in October 1873. In 1875 he gained first-class honours in logic and classics, and again in logic for the following year. In 1877 he won prizes in Persian, Arabic and Hindustani, and graduated LLB (LLD in 1896). In 1876 he was given twelfth place in his first attempt at the Indian Civil Service examination. In 1878 he had another try, passed out eighth, and was posted to the Punjab. This was a great achievement, as at that time the Indian Civil ranked only after the very small Home Civil Service, and my father's family were very strongly against his even attempting the Senior Indian Service – they thought it presumptuous of him! He even had to borrow a hundred pounds from an uncle for his fees and equipment. He told me he got very drunk when the results were out, and celebrating with his friends at the front gate of Trinity he was sick into his top hat.

He went to India in September 1878, aged twenty-two, and

spent two months with his parents and sister in Madras. He joined at Lahore as Assistant Commissioner, and spent his first three leaves in Kashmir shooting big game. He became Assistant Resident in Mysore in 1887, and in the years 1883–5 won prizes for Persian, Arabic, Baluchi, Hindustani and Pushtu (spoken in Afghanistan). Then in 1888 he passed the interpretership in Russian and won a prize of two hundred pounds after a residence of nine months in Moscow. At that time, war with Russia over Afghanistan was thought to be very possible. He was ill after his stay in Russia, and needed rest.

Just at the end of a prolonged leave, his first home leave since he joined the Service, he met my mother in Ireland in 1890. They met just five times, some of them at Enniskerry, by the river Dargle, where my great-grandfather had made his home on retirement. It was love at first sight for both of them. He was thirty-three and she was twenty-three, and must have been quite lovely with her excellent features, wonderful skin and dark gold hair. She was very slim and my father wrote that he would always like her best in the pale grey she was wearing then in mourning for her father. My father was also a very good-looking young man, with fair hair and bright blue eyes.

His leave was at an end all too soon, and mother wrote how she leaned as far as she could out of her bedroom window to see the last of the smoke of his steamer. Their correspondence continued and eventually my father proposed in a letter from Granada. My grandmother insisted on his return for two or three days so that she could see him before giving her consent. He had just reached Rome, having long pre-paid for a short visit to Italy and Greece on his way back to India. However, he hurried back to London for a few days and was warmly approved in August 1890.

My mother's letters to India were pure love-letters, making no mention of contemporary events, or of the spectacular progress of the Harmsworth business. She wrote from Brondesbury, an address she never mentioned at any time to any of her children, I suppose because it marked the lowest ebb of the

Harmsworth family fortunes. It was only after my mother's departure to India that the family moved to 112 Maida Vale, and eventually to 2 Cumberland Place, where the hotel is now.

My father was in debt to the tune of four hundred pounds and was anxious to pay this off before the wedding, which was accordingly delayed till 12 February 1891. Quantities of crested or initialled table glass were ordered from the Army and Navy Stores, and a piano was shipped out to India, though my mother played very little and my father not at all. Alfred (later Northcliffe) gave my mother two hundred pounds for her trousseau, and she travelled out to India with a family friend and was married in Karachi. I still have the reassuring telegram she sent home to her mother on the occasion. It is only one word – 'Married'.

My father was Deputy Commissioner of Dera Ismail Khan from 1890 to 1895, and it was there, or near there, that my two eldest sisters and eldest brother were born. He was Political Officer, Waziristan Field Force in 1894: Boundary Officer, Indo-Afghan Demarcation Commission 1895: Deputy Commissioner, Peshawar 1895–7: Deputy Commissioner, Kohat 1897–1900: Political Officer on the Tirah Expedition 1897–8 – Despatches, medal with three clasps and CSI. Later he was Commissioner in Lahore, Multan and Rawalpindi, finally retiring in 1905. His knighthood was not given him for services in India, but was a present from Rothermere to my mother when Lloyd George was Prime Minister, and in need of Press support. He was stationed in Simla at least in 1903, perhaps in connection with the Salt Revenue, and while there got to know the Viceroy, Lord Curzon, who was godfather to my younger brother. In 1903 my mother, with the younger children, went home to set about finding a retirement job for my father, and he was appointed Professor of Oriental Languages and Reader in Indian History at Trinity College Dublin, occupying the same rooms he and his father had had as undergraduates. On returning home, he sold in Amsterdam his very fine coin collection. So many conquerors have passed through the Khyber

Pass and followed the Indus that he had opportunities of which he made full use. In particular his collection of coins of the 'White Huns' was unique, and is still remembered. Most of his coins were bought at the auction for the Tsar's collection.

My father retired from the Indian Civil Service immediately he had completed twenty-five years' service and qualified for a full pension. He then settled down until his academic retirement in 1920. During this period he worked long hours at his books, and at one time collected Greek coins, but subsequently gave them up and collected prehistoric stone implements. He had a rock garden devoted to a collection of Irish ferns, and looked forward each year to grouse-shooting – in the Dublin hills in the early years, and subsequently in Aberdeenshire, near Aboyne, where my parents eventually settled and where, in due course, they both died.

In thinking of my father I find it impossible to reconcile the picture of the youth with an education in remote County Clare, ambitious, enterprising and brilliant, with the irascible old gentleman I knew, who had no imagination and no enterprise that I ever noticed. When I say irascible, there was an occasion I was told of when he was displeased with the Sunday joint, and threw the leg of mutton out of the window. There was also an occasion, which I vividly recall, when he kicked me down a flight of stairs. When I asked why, I was told I knew full well, but I didn't! I supposed I was making too much noise, but I was a quiet child and this did not seem certain. My mother insisted on my father's being treated with great deference, but we all observed that on family matters she herself ignored him. My sister Enid, who was not often at home, established a warm relationship with him, but for the rest of us he was an old man in the study who played no part in our lives at all.

My earliest recollection is of his playing his last game of tennis. He behaved like an old man, but during the years in Ireland he only went in age from forty-eight to sixty-three. He worked very slowly, up to twelve hours a day, and always looked on me as lazy, as I could not work flat out for more than six, in which time, however, I could get through more than he could in twelve. The contrast between my father in 1878 and my father in, say, 1908, when I can first remember him, is so great that it has always seemed to me that the explanation must be with my mother, who devitalized him and squashed him flat. The Indian climate might have been a cause, but then my father spent his service in the hills of the North-West frontier and not in the plains, which must have been very trying in those days, in great heat with no electric fans and no ice.

I suppose it is now time I entered the scene. I went out to India when I was a small baby and stayed till I was two. At that age my hair was so fair it was almost white, so I was called Snowball, later abbreviated to Snowie. I have no recollection of India or the journey home, though I was told I used to offer to 'whip the tigers off the path'. I shared a bunk with my sister Enid on the voyage home, while my mother and the twins shared a cabin with two ayahs. I fell off the seat on the way home in the PLM train from Marseilles and cut my forehead badly on the heating grid, leaving a scar which was visible for many a long year.

We moved into the Old House, Totteridge, and lived there for two years while my father was still in India. The house was on the opposite side of the road from Poynters Hall, and looks now very much as it did then. My earliest recollections are of Totteridge – my very first is of being held by Nurse Dunch, who gripped my nose while pouring medicine down my necessarily open mouth. I can remember getting my woollen gloves dirty on the pram wheel in which I was being pushed: Aunt Christabel's wedding to Percy Burton: receiving a sovereign from Uncle Alfred (Northcliffe) when he became a peer in 1905: going home from a children's party given by Uncle Harold (Rothermere) and Aunt Lil in such dense fog that the footman had to walk in front with one of the carriage lamps to light the way. Finally, I can remember a visit to Elmwood, Northcliffe's place in Thanet, where there was a boat from an Arctic expedition Northcliffe had financed, and an alligator in the hothouse.

I can remember lying in bed and watching the light from the North Foreland lighthouse light up the ceiling as the beam swept round. It was on this visit that Miss Matthews – I remember her christian names were Amy Janetta – was installed as our governess, which she remained for five years or so. I was too young to join her class at that time, but did so later. Miss Matthews was very short and somewhat hunchbacked, very plain and with pince-nez. We were all rather tall children and towered over her. However, she was a strict disciplinarian and an excellent teacher. What we learned from her we really learned. Though she was one of the earliest women to get a London BA, her pay was only eighty pounds a year, for three terms and the Easter holidays, when my parents were abroad. She always held up to us as a paragon the girl, Nesta, she had taught before, who lived, I remember, at Crowcombe Court. We got very tired of hearing of Crowcombe, but I am grateful for the excellent grounding this woman gave us all.

I remember arriving in Ireland – I think it was November, anyway it was pouring with rain. The twins were dressed alike in bright red. The house to which we came, Roebuck Hall, was to be the family home for fifteen years. It was a large late Georgian house, standing in about eleven acres, and situated about four miles south of the centre of Dublin. At this time the family income was £2,000 a year allowance from Northcliffe, £1,000 a year my father's pension, and £300 a year (I think) from Trinity College – say £3,500 in all, equivalent in purchasing power today to about £15,000 a year free of tax. When my mother let the local agency for domestics know that she wanted a full staff, she was astonished to encounter a queue right down the street on the appointed day when she was to make her choice. Though ours was only a middle-class household by the standards of the day, we had a governess, a cook and kitchen-maid, a parlour-maid, house-maid and between-maid. We had a coachman, two gardeners and a garden boy. We had two walled gardens in which were a hot-house, a large peach and nectarine house, and a vinery. When we arrived we had two horses,

Leila and Majnun, and four carriages, an open victoria, a landau, a closed brougham and an Irish jaunting-car, the latter in black and yellow, very smart. We had a telephone, at that time unusual for private people in Ireland. The apparatus hung on the wall and contained two large batteries, and you wound a handle when you wanted to call the exchange.

Roebuck Hall, when I last saw it some years ago, was used partly for storing Aaron Electricity Meters and partly as a sausage factory. More recently the house has been converted into small flats. The grounds are being covered by new houses and the stables, no longer a sausage factory, are now used for manufacturing an adhesive called 'Stomac'!

Of course Ireland in those days, even the suburbs of Dublin, was very different from Ireland now, or from England then. To start with, the poverty. The children in the streets had no shoes or stockings, summer or winter: the slum women had no shoes or stockings in the summer. At a jumble sale, or other gathering of really poor women, the stench was appalling. Irish people were dirty because they did not have the money for soap. We were constantly reminded of the famine of the 1840s, because the roads round us were lined with walls seven feet high that were built as famine relief. It made our walks very dull as there was nothing to look at except the traffic on the road. We used often to pass a convent of the Immaculate Conception. One day I asked Miss Matthews what an Immaculate Conception was. She said – I am afraid all too optimistically – that I would know when I grew up.

There was also, of course, the agitation for Home Rule, not very prominent when we arrived, but developing as the years went by, culminating in the Easter Rising of 1916. But very early on we used to see our favourite roadman drilling in a field. Even as late as this immediate pre-war period, Ireland was the Ireland of the Protestant ascendancy. Anyone of any social or official position was a Protestant, as they are in Northern Ireland today. The only exception I can remember was Starkie, Enid Starkie's father, who was made head of the Department of Education in Ireland as a conciliatory gesture to the Catholics. The Nationalists were all Catholics, and the forces of law and order were Protestant. Being Protestant, we were vaguely anti-Nationalist, though my father recalled from time to time his Fenian father.

In the years between our arrival in Ireland and my departure to my prep school in 1911, I led a quiet and rather solitary life. My sister Enid, three years older than me, went to school when she was thirteen, and before then used to spend much time at Poynters with my grandmother. My elder brother Lucas, six years older than me, was away at boarding-school and sometimes away in the holidays. The twins, nearly two years younger, were sufficient unto themselves. At first I was in the nursery, where we had a succession of nannies. I can remember one who beat us with canes, and another who beat my naked sister with the prickly side of a hairbrush. A third one, whom we liked, taught us to sing hymns and was dismissed for being sentimental! Perhaps we were too obviously fond of her. In those years my sister Sheila, who was keen on acting, arranged for me to play the part of a Grain of Mustard Seed in the Dundrum parish hall. I had only one word to say, but didn't say it, but instead rolled myself up in the curtain and wept. Not long afterwards I was billed to appear as Cupid, with flesh-pink tights and a bow and arrow. But, mercifully, I caught 'flu and was put to bed, and thus my stage career ended.

The general principle on which I was brought up was, 'Go out and see what little Cecil is doing and tell him not to do it.' I was also reminded of my grandfather's maxim, 'If you have nothing to say, don't say it.'

The weekly thrill for my sisters in winter was Miss Wordsworth's dancing class in the Molesworth Hall in Dublin, premises which remain unchanged from my childhood. It was anything but a treat for me, one of two boys in a large class of girls. I was dressed in navy-blue serge and an Eton collar, with long black stockings over my knees and black patent leather shoes. I was awarded a box of chocolates when, after many months of boredom, I learned to dance the polka. The girls thought this monstrously unfair, as they had learnt in a very few lessons. After the class we had tea in a shop and went home, as we had come, in the landau. It was at this class that I met Enid Starkie, who was at the Alexandra College with my sisters, and with whom I have kept in touch until the present day.

After a period in the nursery I was promoted to the school-room. Of my lessons, I can only remember my first French lesson, 'Le pigeon vole', and my piano lessons. After two years I was still unable to play a little piece called 'Hay-making', so my musical career ended before I reached my prep school.

We were in the parish of Dundrum, and at that time the vicar was a Canon Gibbon, father of Monk Gibbon, quite a noted poet. We didn't often see him as we attended St Thomas's, a very small chapel of ease nearer home. Facing the altar, we were in the front row on the left, while the Nutting family were on the other side. Sir John Nutting was given his baronetcy for bottling Guinness, and his grandson is the Anthony Nutting who sprang into prominence by resigning over Eden's Suez venture. The harmonium was played by a stockbroker called Dudgeon, father and grandfather of very well-known horsemen. We always had a hymn on Christmas Day, 'For the Dying Year'. The words, I can remember, ran, 'Days and moments quickly flying, Blend the living with the dead ... Each within our narrow bed'. This did not strike us children as appropriate Christmas fare. The parson who usually took the service was called Kingsmill-Moore. In one sermon he said children were 'like penguins and young seals'. The King family in the front row, usually well-behaved, burst out laughing and were sharply (but surely unfairly) reproved from the pulpit. A hymn that used to puzzle me was one about Jacob's Ladder. The long climb began on the ladder, but in a verse which I think is not in the usual English hymnal, it goes on: 'Sun, moon and stars forgot, Upwards I fly.' But, surely, at that height there would be no air, and what happened to the ladder?

21

Of this period I remember two parties – one at Kilmainham, the Irish equivalent of Chelsea Royal Hospital, where Sir Neville Wilkinson gave a fancy-dress ball for children. I think I was dressed as Henry VIII, in a hired costume complete with dagger. In the course of the evening I had a quarrel with another boy and attacked him with the knife. We were separated by the General's ADC before any damage was done, but it was the first of three episodes that I can recall when I lost my temper. After the third episode, at Winchester, it was clear that if I allowed this to happen again I should kill someone. So I decided I must never lose my temper again – nor have I. In the other party episode, I was accused of breaking a little girl's necklace, which I denied. However, a fight ensued in the supper-room, in the course of which I hurled a jelly at a small boy. It missed the boy but hit the wall behind him. I can still see the jelly trickling down the wall as the maid came in. She told us off severely, pointing out (to my astonishment) that the wallpaper was not even paid for!

Even at that age, before I went to a prep school, I was criticized by my nurse for preferring the society of little girls to that of little boys. At the age I was then, five to eight, there is said by psychologists to be no sexual element in this, but an anxious search for the mother you haven't had. However that may be, I have always preferred the company of girls and women to that of boys and men, which is why I found boarding-school so hard to take.

When I was the usual sort of age for a prep school my mother fixed on Rose Hill, Banstead, near Epsom. Her reasons for choosing this school – I never heard she looked at any others – was that at Totteridge there were the Alloms. He was a partner in the firm of White, Allom, who were interior decorators. Their son was at Rose Hill, so I was sent there too. My brother Luke had gone to Tyttenhanger Lodge near St Albans, but for some reason this was not considered. Rose Hill, when I went there, had one Browning for headmaster. He was a tall, dark man, but it was his wife who ran the school, a rather cold sort of woman I seem to remember. Though I was at this school for a year and a half, I remember very little about it except my mother in floods of tears as she left me there, and the swimming at Epsom Baths. At the very beginning we were tried for the choir. The new boys were all singing something and the master commented on the extraordinary noise coming from the rear. This proved to be me singing, apparently very out of tune. I have not got a good ear, though I used to be able to whistle rather well. But after this shaming experience I never tried singing again. Of the boys there at that time I remember Frank Vosper, who became quite a successful actor but committed suicide, Brigadier Cross, the secretary of the Commonwealth Press Union, and Jocelyn Hennessy, a free-lance journalist, and the last are the only two old members of the school I can remember meeting in later life.

After four terms I was so thin I was taken away from the school, as our doctor in Ireland said I would die if left there. I don't remember being badly fed, but I was miserable, homesick and a bed-wetter, so my thinness may well have had a psychological cause.

Anyway, on leaving Rose Hill I went to Strangways in Stephens Green, Dublin, almost opposite the Shelburne Hotel. It was a Protestant day school, to prepare boys for Trinity College Dublin. I walked a mile and a half to Clonskeagh, then by tram to Stephens Green, and returned the way I came. The boys were a rough lot and the masters an even rougher lot. We called one the Jervey (Irish for cabby) because his hands were so dirty. There was a grotesque French master always mourning that he had lost his chance of a huge fee. He had translated a legal document and only realized too late that it involved a very large sum of money. He was under the delusion that he could have charged a percentage. Two of the best teachers were women, and the standard of teaching seemed to me better than either at Rose Hill or later at Winchester. The headmaster was a man called Crawford, I think, quiet, competent and rather deaf. It has often been said that women

23

cannot teach adolescent youths; it was certainly not true at Strangways.

Until I went to Winchester in January 1915 I lived at home. I was a voracious reader. By the time I was thirteen I had read more books than most people in a lifetime. My father had a considerable library and my mother and sisters had also large numbers of books. I was and am unable to read poetry, and find it still more difficult to memorize. But at an early age I had read all Dickens, Thackeray, Jane Austen, George Eliot and even Scott, whose novels I found very heavy going: not Trollope, who was almost unknown at that time. In addition to novels, I read translations of the classics, scientific books, books on anything I could lay my hands on. This was not actually disallowed, but was disapproved of.

We were given our first motor-car, a Darracq. Uncle Leicester Harmsworth at that time owned the company and made us a present of his make of car, at that time a great success. The horses and the carriages were sold, but we had a pony-trap with a pony on which I won a prize at the Dublin Horse Show. There were three entrants, of which one was eliminated by a medical inspection and I won the second prize of fifteen pounds. I was not really interested in horses, though I had ridden the carriage horses earlier on. But I was very interested in the motor-car. I was no mechanic – in fact I have no manual gift of any kind, but I was interested in the principle and in our chauffeur, a stage Irishman called Turley. Not only did I spend much time with him while he serviced the car, but we used to comb the slums of Dublin, particularly the Quays, looking for tools and spare parts. I remember once seeing a shopkeeper making signals to his family, and asking Turley what the signals were about. He said the staff were being warned that I was a thief! I asked why I should be thought a thief. Because I was wearing a raincoat, it could only be to conceal my thefts! I was interested in watching the local blacksmith and in cabinet-making. So for a short time I was attached to the blacksmith and later to Hicks, the best cabinet-maker in Ireland at the time. But I

Poynters Hall, Totteridge, as it looked about the time of Cecil King's birth. He was born in one of the rooms at the back looking onto the garden. It was for twenty-five years or so the home of Mrs Harmsworth, his grandmother, and the meeting place of her sons and daughters, particularly Lord Northcliffe. The house has long since been demolished, and the fine oak staircase is now said to be in a house in Morocco.

1905. In the garden of the Old House, Totteridge, which still stands, apparently unchanged. Lady King with Cecil and his sister Enid.

A contemporary fashion note: Cecil King in party frock.

am impossibly clumsy with my hands and this came to nothing. In the west of Ireland there are many whitewashed walls and innumerable donkeys. One day I commented on Turley's collar, which was much too tall. He said, 'Sure, I am like an ass looking over a whitewashed wall.' Motoring in Ireland in those days was very different from now. The roads were macadamized but full of pot-holes. There were few signposts; in dry weather a motor-car threw up an enormous cloud of dust. Speed was about 20 miles per hour; punctures were common; the lubrication of the engine was chancy, and the engine therefore likely to break down; changing gear was difficult; traffic was almost non-existent. I remember Northcliffe telling me in 1919 or so, to my amazement, that in the United States the cars had buffers, and there were signal lights at cross-roads, just as on a railway.

All this time my father continued his academic duties at TCD, mostly teaching candidates for the Indian Civil Service. At TCD he met the members of the Irish literary renaissance, but my mother barely met them and thought the literary stars of the period beneath her socially. I very occasionally lunched with my father and his fellow professors in their lunch-room, and met Gogarty. Mahaffy, the great Greek scholar and Provost of Trinity, came to lunch and I met him several times. My father saw something of James Stevens, author of *The Crock of Gold*. He formed a collection of first editions by modern Irish authors from Le Fanu to James Joyce. The family went occasionally to the Abbey Theatre, but this really exciting period for literature in Ireland passed the King family almost entirely by.

Sometimes I sat behind my father on the bench at Dundrum. He was a JP from 1905, being a Doctor of Laws, and having been a magistrate in India. On one occasion – my only clash with the police in my life – I was caught by a plain-clothes policeman riding my bicycle on a pavement. I subsequently received a summons for 'Driving a carriage – to wit a bicycle – on the public pathway'. The summons ended with the date on which I was to appear in court, and the warning in capital letters 'Herein fail at your peril'. I did appear in court and was fined sixpence.

Life went on at Roebuck. My two elder sisters had coming-out balls. At one of them my mother was considerably put out to find an ear-ring in her bed when the guests had left. My elder brother, after Winchester, distinguished himself at Sandhurst and joined the 60th Rifles in India in 1912. My own interests, apart from reading, lay in chemistry and I used to interest myself with elementary experiments in the harness room of the stables, which was no longer needed for its original purpose. It had gas laid on – the whole house was lighted by gas; there was no electricity. The room was so dirty it was impossible to keep any experiment clean. I don't know why I had this continuing interest in chemistry. When I was at Oxford I thought I could get a second in any subject. Seconds at that time were harder to come by than they are now; most honours degrees were thirds. I thought I might have got a first in chemistry, though in no other subject. I even thought at one time of a scientific career as a research chemist but concluded, quite rightly, that my mathematics would never be good enough.

The staff at Roebuck were almost stage Irish – 'Cookie' the cook, who could read a bit but not write; Calvert the head gardener, northern Irish, so much more competent but less amusing; Donnelly, the other gardener, who used to sing a song of which I can only remember the words, 'Judie and Jack, dressed in black, with silver buttons down their back'; Mackinaspie the window-cleaner, who was usually in gaol when wanted; Maggie the parlourmaid, very hot-tempered – I remember her throwing a basin of washing-up water over me because I had given her a fright; Matilda, who looked after the nursery when we were getting older. She was like so many Nationalists with exaggerated ideas of the benefits of Home Rule. She told us that when Home Rule was established, gold and diamond mines would be opened up all over Ireland. When she died many years later, still in my mother's service, looking after her grandson John Falls, it was revealed that she had always carried a bag of gold sovereigns and half-sovereigns round her waist. I cannot remember how many, seventy pounds' worth perhaps, but certainly a sufficient number to be a considerable weight. She was a shrewd old bird who once said to my mother, 'M'lady, you may be clever but you're not wise.' This did not sound rude in Tilly's brogue and was so true. During this period my elder brother was usually away, at school in the term and with friends in the holidays. Enid was also mostly at school or Poynters, leaving my two eldest sisters and the three youngest at home. Nora was encouraged to play the part of an extra governess. Even if one could escape the notice of mother and governess, there was always eldest sister as a long-stop.

My father had two great friends remaining over from his service in India. One's surname was Angelo, whom I now suppose to have been a homosexual. He was very close to the Leicester Harmsworths at one time, but that relationship came to an abrupt end. The other friend, Colonel Phillott, was a retired colonel in the Indian Army, and a great expert on hawking. Eventually he thought he would like to marry and settle down, but knowing no suitable women, he applied at a matrimonial agency for a widow with some private means. He was rejected out of hand as not having nearly enough to offer a bride with such advantages!

Of course we went on visits to my grandmother Harmsworth, and that is where I got to know the various uncles and aunts.

Towards the end of this time, I was introduced to shooting, originally on the demesne of Lord Massey's park in the Dublin Mountains. At first there were sitting rabbits, but eventually I graduated to woodcock, which came in from Scandinavia in the cold weather. They were damnably difficult shooting; normally one would only see a flicker as they swooped over a rhododendron bush. My first go at grouse shooting was near Aboyne in the autumn of 1914.

In 1914 it was decided that I should try for a Winchester scholarship. My brother had gone to Winchester, though the family had no Winchester connections. I think my parents were against snobbish schools, or perhaps felt they could not aspire so high socially. So it was Winchester and the 60th Rifles for my brother, and not Eton and the Brigade of Guards. Though I did quite well at Strangways, it was a school to prepare boys for entrance to Trinity College Dublin. Winchester scholarships were the object of very special coaching at several prep schools. The examination was a very stiff one, particularly in classics, and I am not a good examinee. However, off I went with my eldest sister to Winchester and, of course, failed. As I was eventually placed in Junior Part 1, while the scholars were placed in Middle Part 1, three whole classes higher, I must have done very badly. The same mistake was made in due course at Oxford. But it all added to the impression ground into me by my parents that I was not any good at anything – that not only would I be a failure in life, but I should find it hard to earn a living of any kind among the fantastically clever people I should encounter. Even to this day, I am astonished when anything for which I am responsible comes out right. However, on the strength of my scholarship attempt I was exempted from the entrance examination and my mother, at very short notice, managed to get me a vacancy.

In the meantime, I enjoyed my first shooting holiday in Scotland. My parents had taken Lumphanan shooting for the season and a house in Aboyne (The Pines). We actually arrived on 5 August 1914. As we were puffing along the coast line from Stonehaven to Aberdeen my father looked out to sea and surmised that a great naval battle might be proceeding. The idea prevalent at that time was that on the declaration of war, the two navies would steam out into the North Sea and, as the British fleet was stronger than the German, we should win. No one stopped to ask why the Germans should do anything so foolish. I cannot remember that the War made any more impact until the following spring, when my brother had returned from India with his regiment and was fighting in France.

I must now try and describe Winchester, where I went in January 1915, as it was in my day, and its impact on me. The house I went to was a mediocre one called Hoppers, after a former housemaster, who was lame. The housemaster in my day was a parson, A. G. Bather. He did not wear a clerical collar but went back to an earlier tradition, a turn-down collar with a white bow tie tucked under it. He had an efficient north-country wife and an only daughter, who more recently was for a time head of the women police in London. Bather himself was keenly interested in Greek and cricket, and anyone who showed promise in either field was sure of his approval. His religious convictions were not evident, and it was said that he kept a stop-watch on the altar and rejoiced when he beat his previous best time for the General Confession, or indeed any prayer. Whether the story was true or false, his religious faith was at best tepid and his impact on his house small. The headmaster was Montague John Rendall, who was a formidable personality and has been described in his biography as a 'great headmaster'. In the four-and-a-half years I was at Winchester he had no relationship of any kind with anyone in my house. There were four hundred and fifty boys in the school, thirty-eight in each of ten houses, and seventy scholars, so to ignore thirty-eight for four and a half years out of so small a number showed a remarkable lack of interest in the ordinary boy. He may have played a part in the lives of a few favoured scholars, but to the ordinary member of the school he was a distant figure-head, very unlike his predecessor, Dr Burge (later Bishop of Oxford), who was said to know by name every boy in the school. Rendall was very interested in Italian art, and was a man of ostentatious piety. The boys thought him a religious humbug. He was certainly in part a humbug, but the boys may have been unfair about the religion. The second master, who is really the housemaster in charge of the scholars, was in my day A. T. P. Williams. He was a pleasant nonentity, with a stone-deaf wife. He triumphed over these handicaps to become headmaster of Winchester, Dean of Christ Church, Bishop of Durham and

Bishop of Winchester. The school worked on the principle that the top half of a class moved up each term: the bottom half stayed put. If after a year a boy was still in the same class, he was sent away. Though it was supposed to be an intellectual school, proficiency in games carried far more prestige than any academic brilliance. The two most important games were Winchester football, played in the autumn term, and cricket. Soccer, played in the spring term, in my view a much better game than either of the others, was not so highly regarded.

I hated almost every day of my time at Winchester and, in any case, my first term was a disaster. I am not a conformist and Winchester was a very conformist institution, so my approach to becoming a Wykehamist was not suitably reverential. I was very homesick, and I think this is worse if you are unhappy at home. A happy home life gives you a secure base from which you can issue with confidence. But if life at home takes all you have got, life at a boarding-school is just the last straw. Apart from having to conform to an elaborate set of rules and customs, many of which seemed to me absurd, we were never allowed to be alone. You had to be with another at all times – one other boy, not two. He had to be of your own seniority and in your own house. This limited you to about ten boys in the whole school. When I say you were never alone, even the lavatories were without doors. I didn't like little boys and I am desperately dependent on being alone part of every day, so daily life at Winchester was very heavy going for me, though the other boys took it all in their stride.

In the course of the first term I developed a cough. The matron (called like all matrons at that time, 'the Hag') said it was a stomach-cough, whatever that may be, and gave me a pill. However, subsequently, playing football in a snow-storm, I collapsed and was taken off to the sanatorium suffering from bronchitis, pneumonia and measles. Almost at once I was put into a small ward with another boy – a sort of death-cell. He died and I just didn't. My main recollection of my stay at the sanatorium was that the night-nurses (the sanatorium was full

when they left school, but Northcliffe did not do so – nor in my turn did I.

Towards the end of his life he had persecution mania – the Germans were after him, and he showed me a secret catch which opened a door that would get him away if he was cornered (I think in his bathroom).

Four final reminiscences of Northcliffe: my grandmother and mother driving home in a cab after Northcliffe's wedding, and Granny Harmsworth in tears, saying to my mother, 'They will have so many children and no money': Northcliffe telling me that he could take a penny bus-ride and return with a story any newspaper would be glad to print; I think this was true, and was a measure of his powers of observation and of his skill as a journalist: Northcliffe saying that the 'Suppress' was so much more interesting than the Press: his telling me there were only two circumstances in which wealth made a real difference, in illness and when travelling.

Geraldine

My mother was the second member of the family. Her relationship was with her father rather than with her mother, who was not fond of girls anyway. She lived all her later life in some awe of Alfred, and played a considerable part in bringing up the younger ones, for whom she never expressed any affection, except for Christabel. I have all the letters my father addressed to her while they were engaged, and though I have not read them, Enid has. She says it was clearly a love relationship, at least until the birth of Nora, after which the letters cease. I was not born until nine years after Nora and, in any case, have no clear recollection of Mother until I was eight or so. By that time it always seemed to me that Mother married for social reasons and really recognized no others. She married when my father was stationed in Dera Ismail Khan, and came home after five years with three children. She enjoyed her time in India and told Enid she wept into her trunk when she was packing to leave for the last time in 1903. Of course, the wife of a senior official in the

Indian Civil Service at that time and place was the social queen of a very large area. Her social position in that area was clearly defined, and in normal times above that of any other woman. This meant an enormous amount to my mother. Her early experiences had given her a sense of social insecurity and her anxiety for Luke and me to join 'good regiments' was because this would guarantee our social position. Even at the end of her life, when my position at the centre of things was socially stronger than any military officer of my age group, she hankered after an official post with a reasonably high and defined position. She had no schooling, but when sixteen or seventeen spent a year with her aunts in Wiesbaden, and a smattering of German remained with her. But I should describe her as very sketchily educated. She was highly intelligent and, like most of her brothers, very amusing at times. She had excellent features, a wonderful complexion, and attractive reddish-brown hair when she was young. It was difficult to carry on a conversation with her as, at least from Luke's death in 1915, her mind was entirely closed, with an outlook on life in many ways untenable.

I was her favourite child, for reasons that escape me. Perhaps it was because I was such a good-looking boy. When Luke was killed in action in 1915, something broke in her. She was in a state of despair. I was at home recovering from a severe illness and had to be with her endlessly. When he was alive she took no interest in him and, in fact, he found his holidays intolerably boring. She had also desperately wanted him to become a regular soldier in spite of the repeated warnings by Northcliffe that a war against Germany was pending. She was normally a dignified and reserved woman, but I can still remember her literally screaming with excitement when the 60th Rifles (which was to be his regiment) marched past in full-dress uniform.

Mother was not a religious woman, but she went to church until Luke was killed though never afterwards, except for weddings, where she normally behaved badly. She thought God had let her down and had no further use for Him. Conversation with her became increasingly difficult as she grew older. She went almost nowhere and did almost nothing. She took no interest in me or my doings, though my existence and attentions to her were important. I looked after her financial affairs, so discussion of stocks and shares was all right. Kind friends said I was interested in nothing but money, when I was desperately seeking some unemotional subject with which to break the silence! Like all the Harmsworths, she deplored my connection with the *Daily Mirror*. Popular newspapers were the source of their wealth, their power and their titles, but they did not want to be reminded of this any more than they wished to be reminded of Brondesbury.

I suppose the principal impressions of my mother left on my mind now, twenty-two years after her death, are the negative nature of her life and her lack of a capacity for love. Jean Jackson, an old friend of the family, first saw Mother in 1896 when Mother was twenty-nine. Asked what impression Mother made, she said Mother was a beautiful woman sitting in a chair doing nothing. I suppose I can remember her from the time she was about forty. She then looked after the household, briefly and firmly. We had three cows or so, and she directed the activities of the cow-man. She saw us children for an hour a day, did a microscopic amount of entertaining, a little mending of her own clothes, and wrote a few letters. Later in life, after we left Ireland, the cows dropped out and nothing took their place. She always said she would have liked to go into politics, but she never took a hand in local affairs when she could have done so, and only took a very superficial and prejudiced interest in national affairs at any time. She said she had always wanted to go to Japan. After 1925 and my father's death, she could have gone at any time with any companion she might fancy, but nothing would induce her to move. I always said that she had inside an irresistible force up against an immovable obstacle. However that may be, she gave out an impression of immense tension. She was no mother to her children and no wife to her husband, but she did not achieve anything at all outside the family circle either. It was a source of constant astonishment to me that anyone with her beauty, her intelligence and her immense force of character could end up with no achievement of any kind.

I used to think the violent emotional force pent up in her was a sexual one, heated by life in India, but frustrated by the very conventional world she lived in. That there was a violent emotional force pent up was obvious on the rare occasions when she lost her temper. She was violently racist and against anyone with a trace of Indian or, even worse, negro blood. When in India, had she been tempted and poured out her frustration in hostile feelings to Indians of all kinds? On three occasions in her life, within my memory, she fell violently for other women. The first occasion was when she was about fifty, and subsequently when she was well over seventy. The ladies in question took it all in their stride, one of them a dull woman who took no interest in Mother anyway. Nevertheless, in spite of these episodes, I doubt whether Mother was Lesbian – and quite certainly not consciously.

The early photographs of Mother show a softness which entirely vanished from her face later in life. She always said to me I was her favourite child, but it was Nora, the eldest, who was always treated quite differently from the rest of us. Were her relations with my father happier when she was conceived than they were later, or what? I think at a later stage Mother was sorry for Nora, who did not marry, and took up with a very unsatisfactory parson and his religious group. But when I first remember Nora she was an attractive girl of sixteen or so, with a wonderful voice, but shy and awkward. She may have been discouraged by the fact that Sheila, the next member of the family, was so much more attractive both in appearance and in character. But there was no obvious reason for specially favourable treatment. It was with Sheila that Mother was at her worst. Sheila was pretty, gay and very attractive, and had had proposals of marriage when she was sixteen, but Mother was socially ambitious. She wanted Sheila to marry a duke, or something, but girls can only marry the men they meet, and the young men of our circle at that time consisted of young military and naval officers, whom Mother denounced as beneath Sheila's notice. After a series of shattering rows, Sheila was in a mood to marry anyone to get away from home and, in fact, married a bumptious little naval officer who was the least attractive of her various suitors. However, she died in childbirth before the marriage could come to grief – a terrible loss to me, though it is some consolation that in due course I brought up her grandchildren.

Looking back on my life I feel as if I were an orphan brought up by step-parents, a stepfather who was completely null and a stepmother who was loveless, capricious and occasionally cruel. In fact, the lack of a mother is what I still frequently and strongly feel. As I think I said earlier, I was important to my mother as an extension of herself, but she never took any interest in my character and, in fact, had no idea what sort of person I was. It has seemed to me that I realized as a very small child or baby that my mother would destroy me if I let her. So I developed a most elaborate defensive mechanism that I cannot even now altogether throw off. As an attachment can be used to hurt you, you must have none. Scents and sounds can rouse dangerous feelings that may not be controllable. Cut them out. Sight is more unemotional, so develop it and use it as a defensive weapon. And so on.

I wrote to Enid some years ago of Mother, 'Her attitude to her children in general was immense pride coupled with fairly consistent disapproval of everything they did. She always gave the impression that I was her favourite child, while at the same time giving me no assurance of goodwill or even interest, such as is accorded by almost every mother to almost every child. In particular, when growing up, just when one's self-confidence needs every help, she was always jeering at my cockerel-like qualities. Even in my case she wanted me to join the Foreign Office or the Army (financial and social security again) and was definitely hostile when I chose to go into the family business. This hostility was maintained throughout her life – she knew nothing of my business career and cared less, and what she could not avoid knowing she vigorously denounced.'

A favourite ploy with my mother was to clean my ears with a handkerchief and a hairpin. This was often very painful and, I thought at the time, intended to be so. She also on occasion thrashed me with her walking-stick, coming to the bathroom afterwards when I was in the bath to inspect the weals.

A last episode. Ten years after my mother's death, when I was fifty-four, I woke up in a panic, having dreamt she was still alive! I had been a good son in outward behaviour, but I must have hated her. I have no wish to do anything with my hands and it has seemed to me over the years that this was because in early childhood I had wanted to strangle her with them.

My mother had a heart attack in 1945, when she was seventy-nine. She had plumped rather heavily into a chair when out playing bridge, and the chair had gone over backwards. I went up to Scotland to be with her but left when she seemed to be all right for the present. However, she later took a sudden turn for the worse and it became obvious that she had only a few hours left. She was well aware of this and not in any way daunted. She sat up in bed, reading *The Times* and dictating arrangements for the funeral to my sister, Chirrie, over the top of the paper.

Harold

Harold (later Rothermere) was the third member of the family, probably handicapped by being the next son in age to North-cliffe, who was so much better looking and so much more attractive in character. He was at the Marylebone Grammar School, but I imagine his schooling was pretty superficial. He was an ugly man, with a powerful kind of bulldog look about him in later life. From photographs as a young man he was much better looking but never had the charm of North-cliffe. My mother used to say what a shy youth he was. When they went to dances, he used to hang about the door saying, 'When can we go?' From school he went into the Board of Trade where he worked as a clerk. I seem to have been told that

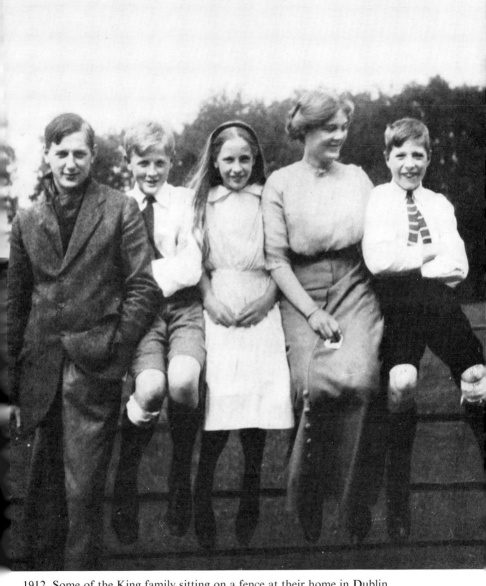

1912. Some of the King family sitting on a fence at their home in Dublin.
From left to right Lucas (killed at Ypres in 1915), Cecil, Geraldine
(one of the twins) now Mrs. Spencer, Nora, the eldest of the family;
Bobby (the other twin), drowned in the *Leinster* when it was torpedoed
in the Irish Channel in 1918.

1916. In the garden at Roebuck Hall. Cecil King with his father, at that time Professor of Oriental Languages at Trinity College, Dublin. The deodar tree behind is still standing.

he worked in a rat-infested basement and that there was an exciting episode when a panic-stricken rat dashed up the inside of his trouser-leg and was caught. Very early on he was taken into Northcliffe's publishing business. He bought the paper and string: my mother went to the British Museum Library for *Answers*, while Northcliffe looked after the editorial. He received a chunk of shares in the Amalgamated Press, in the Associated Newspapers and in the *Daily Mirror*. At a later stage he also owned the *Glasgow Record* and the *Leeds Mercury*. Some of his shares were sold to Sir John Ellerman who, by the time of Northcliffe's death, was a large shareholder in the family companies, as his son still is in the International Publishing Corporation. I don't know when Harold started gambling on Wall Street, but this he presumably did with the money he got from selling some of the family shares. I always heard his principal interests were in Canadian and American public utilities. Anyway, A. S. Fuller, his confidential secretary, told me that by 1926 his holdings were worth twenty-six million. He was thus a far richer man than Northcliffe. It was always said that the two brothers perfectly complemented each other, and that while one ran the editorial side, the other looked after the business. Harold told my mother after North-cliffe's death that of course Alfred owed everything to him, and that without his business management Northcliffe would never have been heard of. I worked on the *Daily Mail* immediately after Northcliffe's death and worked for nine years on the *Mirror* under Rothermere. No one could say Northcliffe was an efficient business manager, but in spite of this the business flourished. In the *Mirror*, in my day, every conceivable blunder was committed, commercial and editorial. I remember saying to John Coope that we had had the finest possible training in how not to run a newspaper. People said that after the death of his two elder sons, Rothermere just didn't care any more, and that his irresponsibility originated in despair. This may be part of the explanation, but I don't think it would account for a very good manager becoming a very bad one, which he certainly was in the period 1923–42 when I was in a position to judge. So I listen with some scepticism to the reports of his brilliant management prior to 1914.

He married in 1893 Lilian Share. According to Guy Bartholomew her father started life as a blacksmith in Shoe Lane. Bart's mother taught singing, and one of her pupils was Lilian. Geoffrey Harmsworth thought Share was a small builder in Norwood, but the machinery for the Geraldine Press in the early days was bought from Share & Co., so presumably Harold met his bride over purchases of printing machinery from papa. I asked Esmond (now Lord Rothermere) whether that is how they met, but he had never heard of the deals in printing machinery. Lil was very pretty, with wonderful blue eyes, and apparently only interested in fashion and make-up. She complained that he called in his secretary to talk business at breakfast the morning after the wedding. He protested that later the same day he gave her one of the finest pearl necklaces in Europe. Anyway, she produced three sons and then refused to have any more children, greatly to Harold's sorrow, because he wanted a large family. I only saw her twice, once at a children's party she gave when I was four, and later in 1916 or so when she arrived late for the memorial service for her eldest son who had died of wounds. At the children's party, a thick pea-soup fog gathered and I remember driving home in a carriage with the footman walking in front holding one of the carriage lamps. She left Harold before the First War and lived in France, where the family always spoke of her as promiscuous and frivolous. However that may be, she financed both Gide and T. S. Eliot when they were both quite unknown. To spot one might be a lucky chance, but these two had little in common, and to have spotted two such literary winners must surely indicate perception of no ordinary kind. But I have never heard any member of the family comment on this. She also persuaded Harold to finance the ballet when it first came to London in the twenties with Diaghilev.

In 1906 she was having an affair with St John, according to

Northcliffe the one of his brothers most like himself. He was being driven home to Poynters after being with her, and his chauffeur was following the telegraph wires because there was a ground fog. Unfortunately, at one point, they took a short cut and left the road. The car, following the telegraph wires, ran up the bank and turned over. St John's back was broken and he spent the next thirty years in an invalid chair paralysed from the waist down.

Rothermere had bought the *Daily Mirror* from Northcliffe in 1914 and had started by dismissing all the circulation reps, including Freddy Poke, the ablest man he ever employed, who afterwards made himself a fortune, of which £800,000 came from *Everybody's Weekly*. Presumably because of the Glasgow and Leeds papers he owned, Rothermere was given a baronetcy in 1910 by the Liberals, but his dabblings in politics only began later under Lloyd George, and when he had bought control of the *Daily Mail* from Northcliffe's executors. I remember Rothermere saying how Lloyd George had asked him if he had any relations in the Church. Rothermere said he hadn't, but why the question? Lloyd George said he had a couple of deaneries vacant that Rothermere might have liked! How typical of Lloyd George to use deaneries as a means of getting or keeping Press support, in that case of the *Daily Mail*!

Rothermere was an incredibly inept politician. Perhaps because Lloyd George had a very keen sense of the importance of the Press, Rothermere had acquired an exaggerated impression of what could be done. Rothermere's and Beaverbrook's attacks on Baldwin were so foolishly conducted that they probably saved him when his party would very properly have thrown him out. We had 'Hats off to Hungary' and something similar on behalf of France, causes that had no echo in the hearts of *Daily Mail* readers. He seemed to regard politics as similar in kind to Stock Exchange speculation. You could switch your support to Hungary or to France, to Mosley, or against him, without any consistent purpose. His enthusiasm for Hungary was said to be due to an attachment to a princess, who was widely believed to be a German spy. His enthusiasm for Hitler was deplorable. One of the German magazines has recently published facsimiles of letters and telegrams from Rothermere to Hitler of a most embarrassingly sycophantic kind. I think Rothermere was a most forceful, able man, disgusted by the ineffectiveness of governments between the wars, hence his contempt for Baldwin and his admiration for Mussolini and Hitler. At least these last got something done. I really think that was about all there was to it. His political senses were vestigial, so he neither saw how to get results at home, nor foresaw the military menace of Hitler.

I think one has to look on Rothermere as a very unhappy man. His life was a failure, and after the death of his two elder sons he devoted himself to fighting off despair. So he plunged into money-making on a great scale. He was ambitious to be the richest man in the country, but thought (he told me) that he never got further than No. 3. The two richest in the middle twenties he thought were Sir John Ellerman and Lord Derby. For a short time in the First War he was Secretary of State for Air. I remember his saying he had cleared out several hotels full of 'carpet knights'. He came up against Trenchard, of whom he had no opinion at all, and the death of his two sons at about that time deprived him of any wish to fight, and he resigned. I cannot believe he would have made a good Minister, as he was inarticulate and no administrator.

My knowledge of my uncles was from meeting them at Poynters when I was staying there, apart, that is, from hearing about them from different members of the family. Northcliffe was very often at Poynters, Rothermere very seldom, so I really saw very little of him until Northcliffe's death. My mother was closer to Northcliffe than any of her other brothers, except perhaps Cecil, but she had almost no relations at all with Rothermere. I think in later life Rothermere had really nothing to live for and took refuge in drink, very crude womanizing, and making money. I never saw him the worse for drink, nor heard of any episode of that kind, but his death was due mainly to cirrhosis of the liver, and his face, certainly for the previous twenty years, had shown signs of excessive drinking. Among his mistresses I can recall a secretary who used to clatter away at her typewriter wearing a ring containing a diamond the size of a pigeon's egg. Evidently she became a nuisance, and Geoffrey Harmsworth told me Rothermere offered him ten thousand a year to marry her! Then there was another lady by whom he had a daughter. But most of his affairs were one-night stands with girls who were astonished to receive mink coats or diamond brooches for their services. He bought a big house in Kent, Benenden, now a girls' school. My mother stayed there once and complained that though forty thousand had been spent on the house and marble doors installed in the bathrooms, it was impossible to get a hot bath. He had other houses, in Dornoch, in Sunningdale, in Avenue Road and at Holt, in Norfolk, but no attempt was made to make any of them a home. I remember calling on him one morning at his suite in the Savoy Hotel. He told me he had slept on the small and uncomfortable sofa in the sitting-room because the bedroom was so noisy – and this was at a time when he had all the money in the world!

He once told me that old mistresses were much more expensive than Old Masters, and he had plenty of experience of both. He liked surrounding himself with rogues, perhaps so as to keep his hand in by getting the better of them. However that may be, the art critic on the *Daily Mail* and one of his own advisers was Konody, a well-known rogue. He advised Rothermere to purchase for eleven thousand pounds a half-length portrait of a Dutchman by Van Dyck. It is given a full page in the printed catalogue of Rothermere's collection. In due course, it descended to me. I didn't like the picture, which I thought was badly painted, notably the hand the sitter had put on his chest. At Sotheby's the picture director said it would fetch about eight hundred pounds if the dealers thought it was by Van Dyck (it was signed!), seventy pounds or so if they did not. It actually fetched three pounds ten, which was much less than the value of the frame.

77

Harold Rothermere was kind to Sonny Harmsworth, the eldest son of Hildebrand. He took a great fancy to him and took him everywhere. There came an occasion when Sonny wrote Rothermere a birthday letter, which pleased – or amused – Rothermere very much. So he decided, he told us, that he should be a baronet, and got Lloyd George to make Hildebrand one. Hildebrand had never done a stroke of work in his life. So when the baronetcy was announced the family inundated him with sarcastic telegrams on the lines of, 'At last a grateful nation has given you your due reward'. Hildebrand himself lived in a small hotel in Hove. He claimed that by standing on a chair one could just see the sea from the window of one of the maids' bedrooms! Anyway, on the day the baronetcy was announced, he strode into the dining-room and said to the waiter, 'Waiter, bring me something fitting for my rank and station: bring me a cold rice pudding.'

Arising from his interest in the Russian ballet Harold became attached to one of the ballerinas. He carried her off on some Continental trip and they were installed in a large suite, but to her indignation, nothing happened!

Rothermere's morale depended apparently on his immense success in making money. But in the slump in 1929 he was a bull, and lost forty million dollars in one month. Subsequently, his attempts to establish the dominant chain of provincial papers was an expensive failure, and during the thirties I think he was dependent on the proceeds from a Canadian and a South African trust fund. Anyway, when he died in 1940 he left about £300,000, which, after death duties, was insufficient to pay the legacies. He was not a man of integrity and used his newspapers to boost the shares of the *Daily Mirror* so that he could sell out. He was confident the paper would cease publication. In 1934 the sale of the *Mirror* was about 730,000 and falling. The *Sunday Pictorial* had lost a million sales in ten years. The outlook was so bleak that I had an opportunity to take my chance.

78

One day he took the most bizarre fancy to his first cousin once removed, Judith Wilson, the younger daughter of Adelaide Bell and her husband, a music teacher in Dublin. She was a plain and uneducated Irish woman of about thirty, just half his age, but very good-natured, easy-going and cheerful. Uncle Harold almost adopted the family and brought them over from Ireland, installing Judith and her parents in a luxury flat on Campden Hill, and finding a job on the Stock Exchange for their son-in-law who was working for Guinness. The father and Meriel, the elder sister, died shortly afterwards and then my Cousin Adelaide and daughter Judith moved into Uncle Harold's house at Virginia Water, where they occupied the most extraordinary position as hostesses, and yet having nothing to do with the running of the grand house.

We had known the family well because they lived in Dublin, and the two cousins, Judith who was my age and Meriel, who was Enid's, used to come to Roebuck to spend Sunday afternoon with us. We thought them very dull, and the best thing about them was Judith's very bright blue eyes.

Uncle Harold was bored with and sometimes very rude to Adelaide, but she was a sort of chaperon, and together these women made a shadowy semblance of a home for him. He lavished jewellery of enormous value on them both, as well as shares and pictures. Judith bequeathed her Boudins to the National Gallery. They seemed to spend their time at one of the most exclusive fashion houses, or endlessly flipping over the pages of the *Tatler*. Judith seemed very nice, quite honest and very dull, a contrast perhaps to his usual entourage.

Enid travelled to Italy with them and Uncle Harold at his invitation in 1934, but could not really understand Judith's and Harold's relationship. They appeared to be lovers, with their fondlings and sloppy baby talk as she sat, an uncomfortable gooseberry, in one of Uncle's two Rolls for mile after mile of Italian countryside; sometimes they would disappear for the whole day, and yet she couldn't quite believe that they had

79

completely committed themselves. The family betting was fifty-fifty.

After some six years, he seemed to join them less and less and the thing just faded out. Christabel said that as soon as he was free in 1937 he wired to Judith proposing marriage, but she refused. I imagine this was because by then there was nothing left in it to make it worth while except material and social advantages, which wouldn't interest Judith (to her honour), and she was by then very rich anyway.

Uncle Harold died in Bermuda in 1940. Judith continued to live with her mother until she died, and then shared an exquisite small manor house with Edith Evans, the actress. They lived separately when in London. Judith died in 1960. Edith Evans told me that until Judith's death she had no idea of her relationship to the Harmsworths.

Cecil

The third son and fourth child was my godfather Cecil, after whom I was called. He was very good-looking, his charm in some way enhanced by a slight cast. He was the best educated of the family, having done well at Trinity College, Dublin, where he was sent at the expense of a family friend. In the early days he played a small part in the Amalgamated Press, but when I can remember him he was a rich man living on his dividends and leading the life of a minor politician. He was for years Liberal MP for Droitwich and subsequently for Luton. Eventually, he was Under-Secretary of State at the Foreign Office under Balfour and finally, I think, Minister in charge of the blockade after the end of the First War. I imagine he could speak quite well in a traditional way, but he had no drive or initiative. I remember Rothermere telling me he was just a punctured tyre. He married a cousin, Emily Maffett, who is reported to have wooed him by sitting with her arms round his neck until he proposed. Though regarded by her friends and her needy relations as a model of generosity and kindness, she always seemed to me a sinister figure. Her first two children died, it was said of neglect, one having been bathed in the sea when only a few days old. Anyway, the family were so incensed by the treatment of these children that my mother, who was on the point of returning to India, was deputed to tell Emily that any further ill-treatment of her children would lead to her being turned away from the doors of the entire family. I doubt whether this had any effect, but the next three children survived, and Emily's hatred of my mother continued till her death. She was always hovering around death-beds, and her friends said, 'How unselfish!', but she always seemed to me to take a ghoulish interest in such occasions.

We lived in Ireland and, Cecil being my godfather, I often spent a night at 28 Montagu Square, or in their house at Henley on my way to and from school. Cecil was very friendly towards me and told mother how pleased he was when, at Winchester, someone took me to be his son. Tem, as she was called, on the other hand regarded me merely as a belonging of the hated Geraldine. Our lack of rapport was enhanced by her behaviour, which at the time seemed to me undignified, struggling on the sofa with young officers, or wandering about the upper floors in her undies. There may have been a sexual angle to all this, but I never heard there was. The only excuse made on her behalf which seemed to me to have any substance was that she had some kind of ear trouble and was in constant pain. Cecil was given a peerage in 1939, by Chamberlain, at Rothermere's instigation. I could never understand this event. Rothermere's support by that time was valueless, and Cecil had dropped out of public life more than fifteen years earlier, not to add that if he deserved a peerage, there were some hundreds of thousands of others equally worthy. Tem died in 1942, and Cecil's existence continued, buttressed by a considerable alcoholic intake. He was intelligent and a great charmer. Perhaps the fact that he achieved nothing could be ascribed to his unpleasant little wife, to whom he was devotedly attached, quoting her on every occasion to audiences who could not have been less appreciative. To revert to his relationship with me: he paid for me to go to Oxford, but was one of the more hostile members of the family to the new *Daily Mirror*. I think I should have expected to be an executor of his will and to have had a small legacy. In fact I was not mentioned, which was quite out of keeping with our earlier ante-*Mirror* relationship. After the War, he even refused to put me up for the Reform Club on the grounds that I was not a Liberal! The Reform at that date would indeed have been a desert if membership had been confined to Liberals.

Leicester

Leicester was the fourth son and fifth child. He was called after a family friend, one George Robinson, engineer to the local gas company, who lived at Stoneygate, Leicester. He was definitely Harmsworthian in appearance, but rather let the side down. The other brothers were all good-looking in a bucolic sort of way, but Leicester, while unmistakably one of them, was very unattractive with a white pudgy face and wispy moustache, and always dressed in black. He originally decided to become a celibate clergyman, spending hours on his knees as a youth, and this was his continued intention, as far as the family knew, when they found a prayer-book inscribed, 'With love from Annie'. However, he soon announced that he had married Annie and that she was expecting a child (Alfie, the eldest of the Harmsworth grandchildren). Annie Scott was apparently the sister of the billiard-marker at the saloon where Leicester played billiards. This game had a great vogue at that time and several of the Harmsworth brothers were very skilled performers. She was a short, dark, common little woman who produced a large family, four sons and two daughters I can remember, but another son may have died young. Leicester's health was never good. He was said to have had rheumatic fever as a child. He, too, was in the family business at the beginning and until 1906, and was given a block of shares. He must have sold these, because by 1910 he had made a fortune in France out of Darracq motor-cars. In spite of his rather ostentatious piety he seems to have been a great gambler. The motor-car fortune went, and at one time he was so 'broke' that my mother undertook to educate the youngest son, Geoffrey. However, in due course, he recovered and made a fortune out of Middle East oil, I think in Egypt. This time he was not going to put it all at risk. He settled money on the family, bought the evening papers in Plymouth and Exeter, and set about making a great collection of books published in English before 1640. His collection was the last great book collection. It would not be possible to get together a collection of that size and quality today. The best part of it was bought by the Foulger Library and is now in Washington. Though unattractive and sanctimonious, he had great ability. Among his other gifts was a great feeling for antiques and works of art. I remember at his house, Moray Lodge, on Campden Hill, bought cheap with some acres in the First War, he had Fantin Latour pictures all up the back stairs. When I saw them, in the early twenties, they were not very highly regarded, but even so seemed cheap at the price of fifteen or twenty pounds, which is what he had paid for them. Many years later one of these pictures went for six thousand pounds. He was a Liberal politician of no distinction, representing Caithness and Sutherland for twenty-two years. I have no idea how he was adopted for such a distant Scottish constituency as he had, so far as I know, no Scottish connections of any kind. His baronetcy in 1920 was presumably partly due to long service in the House of Commons and partly to the influence exerted by his papers. He was quite a genial uncle, but at home was a grim restrictive tyrant, or so I always heard.

Geoffrey told me that after his father died, Harold, his brother, was sitting in his office in Fleet Street, when round the door came a face remarkably like his own. He said, 'Who are you?' and the face replied, 'Your brother', and this was how the family learnt that many years before, Leicester had committed bigamy in his constituency and got clean away with it. The illegitimate son died soon after, leaving no issue.

In 1920 Leicester bought for my grandmother Hill Lodge,

Campden Hill. It was a charming Regency house on two floors. It had a large garden, on part of which four small houses have since been built. Leicester secretly bought and furnished this house and equipped it completely down to the dish-cloths in the kitchen. He introduced a familiar picture here and there, so that it shouldn't seem too strange, and this he did because for years Granny had said how much she would like a house in London where her sons could pop in and out so easily and she could feel near them. But the effort to look for a house and do it up at eighty or so always put her off. When it was at last ready after months of preparation, Uncle Leicester gave it to her and she hated it. She stayed there miserably for about six weeks and then pounced on the opportunity of lending it to my parents, who were on the point of leaving Ireland. Granny never returned, and the house and contents were sold to Esmond, who himself parted with it soon after. Northcliffe was heard to protest at the 'selfishness' and 'presumption' of Leicester in making such a plan, which was a sweet thought for a son to have for his old mother, and no more delightful country house could have been found in London at that time.

Leicester was harsh to his eldest son Alfie, who was never very confident, and was castrated when terribly wounded on his first day in the trenches in France. In the early 1960s he was still living in the huge Manor House at Bexhill. Though he was alone and the house had eleven bathrooms, he used every week to take towel and soap over to the chauffeur's cottage where his mother lived in her middle nineties. Sustained by the brandy bottle, she was provided with two maids and a bathroom that worked.

Hildebrand

Hildebrand, who came next to Leicester, was one of the less attractive members of the family. He was in the Amalgamated Press until 1905 and left about the same time as Leicester. They were each entitled to one-sixth of the profits over £150,000, which may well have been a very substantial sum. They may have left because life with Alfred became increasingly uncongenial. For a period Hildebrand owned the *Globe* evening paper, at a time when there were about nine evening papers in London. He was no newspaper executive and lost £80,000 on the venture. Hildebrand – I never heard why he was so called; was it after the great medieval Pope? – was very Harmsworthian to look at, with a common voice, a considerable wit, eccentricity bordering at times on mental instability, lazy but shrewd. Apart from his *Globe* purchase, I never heard of his doing anything. He accumulated shares in the family businesses and invested heavily in Imperial Tobacco and British American Tobacco. When he died of cirrhosis of the liver it was immediately before the great slump of 1929–30. His shares were valued for probate at the price prevailing on the day of death, but were only sold for death duties later when the price was much lower. As a result, a fortune of £1,600,000 was almost wiped out. Merton College, Oxford got some money for scholarships, and the family ended up with rather little. He married a lady he was said to have picked up on Brighton front and who lived, like some of the other Harmsworth wives, well into the nineties. She was a quite nice, nondescript woman who for many years had her mother living with her. She produced four sons, of whom the youngest, Anthony, a barrister, was the only one to make any kind of a name for himself.

Hildebrand was mostly noted round the family for his strange behaviour, betting the children's nurse five pounds that she couldn't carry the baby round the billiard table fifty times in a given number of minutes. He was offended because his neighbour in his house at Lancaster Gate would sing in her bath, so he paid the servants one week-end, when he was away, to play the gramophone with its horn pressed to their sitting-room wall night and day from Friday to Monday. I remember his saying that people said that as he was a rich man he should have a steam yacht, but he said, 'I hate steam yachts and I like going to the sixpenny enclosure at the Hove Albion football ground on

Saturday afternoons, and that is what I shall continue doing.'

He was educated at Dublin High School by Maffett relatives and subsequently went up to Merton, hence the legacy, but to meet he was not an educated man – uncouth and eccentric would be the impression left on first acquaintance, I should think. Enid said he looked and spoke like a bookie with a purple face and brown boots. She also said his wife sent for her mother in the middle of the honeymoon.

Violet

The next member of the family was Violet. My grandmother, in a fit of exasperation, once said she should have had an extra letter to her name, she should have been christened Violent! She was my godmother, but certainly from my adolescence pursued me with all the malice at her command. This may have been a reflection of her bad relations with my mother. At any rate, I never knew of any other cause.

Violet was born in 1873 and lived on till 1960. She was a coarser, more violent edition of my mother, though not more forceful. She was good-looking in a florid sort of way, lazy, selfish and greedy. At the age of thirty-five she married a very good-looking regular officer in the Northumberland Fusiliers. One of her brothers commented that Wilfred deserved the VC for his temerity in proposing! He came of a well-off family. He had a thousand a year of his own, and that before the First War. His brother became Bishop of Newcastle, and the Northumberland Fusiliers was at that date a 'good' regiment, i.e. the officers had a good social standing. He was one of the stupidest men I ever met, given to lecturing me on education at a time when I was doing well at Winchester, while he had to enter the Army via the Cavan Militia, a body I have not otherwise heard of. He failed to get into Sandhurst. I once stayed in their house for a night. The only book in a large house was an out-of-date copy of the Army List.

Enid described Violet as greedy, crafty and unscrupulous.

86

Granny's butler, who saw more of her than most, said she was a 'vile lady'. No one could stand up to her when she was on the war-path, usually in pursuit of some advantage, for instance Granny's discarded Rolls at eight o'clock on the morning that her new one was due, or a house which Christabel had chosen for herself. Rothermere seems to have enjoyed her manoeuvres. 'What is old Vi up to now?' he would say when she appeared at Poynters looking unduly smart. Her objective was normally to get something of financial value from him. Prior to visits to Poynters, she would save up her letters to post, as Granny supplied free stamps for her drawing-room writing table. Enid remembered her playing bridge, endlessly telephoning her stockbroker, chain-smoking the while. Every winter before the First War she went to Monte Carlo, and would be waiting for the Casino to open every morning at eleven.

Much of family politics originated in the fact that it was she who warned Rothermere that Lil was having an affair with his young brother St John. She used this supposed service as a means of gouging more money out of Rothermere for many, many years afterwards. This was an effect, though, rather than a cause, of the total lack of family solidarity. With the Harmsworths it was all against all.

Two final items. She came out in the nineties for a London Season and drove a phaeton. When she was fifteen, in a violent temper, she sat on the floor and kicked a pair of shoes to pieces.

Charles

The next child was Charles. I saw him only once. He was what I suppose is now called a high-grade mental defective. He was quite normal to meet but could never learn to read or write. Granny was bitterly ashamed of giving birth to Charles and would not have even his existence recorded in any book of reference. By the time I knew anything of the family he was living at Hassocks in Sussex with his faithful companion called, I think, Ringrose. They ran together a little poultry farm, or at any rate amused themselves keeping poultry. He was very

Harmsworthian in appearance, with a terrific cockney accent derived from his companion. From any accounts I heard, he led a very quiet, contented life, ignored by most of the family, including my mother, but not by Granny and not by Christabel.

St John

St John was universally known in the family as 'Bonch'. Northcliffe once told me that Bonch was more like him than any of the other brothers. By the time I knew Bonch, there seemed little resemblance, at any rate on the surface. He was good-looking, very good with people, especially women, a good athlete, elegant and witty. He was in the family business for a few years, but he never received the block of shares dished out to the elder brothers. As I have said earlier, he was crippled in a car accident in 1906 when he was in his upper twenties. From then on he was condemned to an invalid chair, with marriage out of the question. At the time of the accident he was engaged to be married to a Miss Ward, subsequently Lady Barclay, and now Lady Vansittart. He seems to have been devoted to her, as when he died in the thirties, more than thirty years later, she was one of the residuary legatees.

As an undergraduate at Christ Church, wandering round Provence, near Nîmes, he came upon an ancient therapeutic spring in the orchard of a Dr Perrier. There was a muddy pond with natural gas bubbling up, and a few bathing boxes round it, while quite near was a spring of beautifully clear water. He conceived the idea (this *was* like Northcliffe) of pumping the natural gas into the spring water to make a sparkling table water. Bonch was no businessman, and the Source was always under-capitalized and always losing money. However, Bonch never lost faith in his enterprise, and the brothers forked out. When Bonch died, it was sold by his executors for £100,000 to Govett, the stockbroker. It was eventually resold to a French group and is now a very big business indeed. The well-known shape of the bottles was chosen by Bonch from a pair of Indian clubs he had lying in a corner of his room, and the design of the

1919. Cecil King at Oxford. He was at Christ Church from 1919 to 1922, and among his contemporaries in the College were Anthony Eden, Sir Alec Douglas-Home, Henry Luce, and Prince Paul of Yugoslavia.

1930. Out on the moors at Cushnie, Aberdeenshire. From left to right, Herbert Stokes (brother-in-law), Basil Burton (first cousin) and Cecil King. For thirty years he owned the Cushnie estate, and enjoyed the mixed bag obtainable on his mainly grouse-shooting property.

1952. Cecil King, now Chairman of the Daily Mirror which was founded by his uncle, places a wreath on the memorial in Fleet Street to commemorate the 30th anniversary of Northcliffe's death.

label was also his. At one time he built a bottle factory at Aigues-Mortes, but that had to be closed. At one period, I suppose after the First War, extensions were being undertaken and there were Italian workmen on the site. It was said long afterwards that one of the workmen was Benito Mussolini. Years later, when Mussolini was Dictator of Italy, Rothermere asked him if this was true. He said it was – his job had been with a barrow, shifting concrete.

Though paralysed and with almost useless, wasted hands, Bonch was most attractive to women and always had some around. His elder brothers groaned, as they not only supported his business, but also his entourage of masseur, private doctor, valet, chauffeur, and two nurses. He had a special Rolls-Royce ambulance made in which he travelled the countryside, and this mobile court was said to have cost £10,000 a year, even before 1914. If a cutting-down was threatened, he cried – and in front of Granny – and all was restored. I think he could fairly be described as brave and gay, with elegance and good taste, but entirely untrustworthy.

He was popular with the younger members of the family, but for some reason I was never approved. This lack of approbation was enhanced when I once paid a brief visit to a house he had taken for the holidays at Totland Bay in the Isle of Wight. I had gone up about tea-time to have a bath, but it flowed very slowly, so I came down to the sitting-room where tea was brought in. Somewhat later, a large drop of water fell from the ceiling, followed by others. Puzzled at first, I soon realized that my bath (which I had forgotten) had overflowed. I was told subsequently that the ceiling had come down. I was very young at the time, but a deep impression was made, and I was never asked again.

He died in France, but left a request in his will that he should be cremated and his ashes scattered on the sea, midway between England and France, the two countries with which he had had such close connections. To carry out his wishes, a cross-Channel steamer was hired and the family gathered on board in top-hats and tail-coats. Mercifully it was a calm, foggy day, but I couldn't help wondering what would have happened in rough weather! Anyway, we steamed out into the middle of the Channel, a wreath lashed to an inflated inner tyre tube was launched and a tin cigarette box of ashes was scattered down wind. Leicester Harmsworth told one of the family that he was too ill to be on board the boat (he had a weak heart), so he had established himself on an appropriate cliff to watch the proceedings through a telescope! Unfortunately, owing to the fog, he saw nothing.

Christabel

One of my very earliest recollections was being at the wedding of Christabel to Percy Burton at Totteridge Church in 1905. She was one of the least gifted members of the family, and he was good-looking and charming in a very Irish sort of way, but lacked anything more. They went to live at the old house just opposite Poynters. The house belonged to Granny and we had just left it to settle in Ireland. Percy had started up an advertising agency, P. C. Burton & Co., which was afterwards absorbed by the St James Agency, itself to be absorbed later by the London Press Exchange. Christabel had been closer to my mother than any of her brothers or her other sister, and being so much younger, she was nearer in age to my older sisters. She was also in and out of Poynters every day when we were staying there, so on every ground we knew Christa best of all our Harmsworth uncles and aunts. You couldn't dislike her. She was kind and friendly, but lacked brains or any sort of drive, judgement or purpose. Enid likened her to a large red jelly! She was sloppy, always ready to find excuses for anyone or anything. Percy Burton was a pleasant extrovert, just the man for the early days of advertising. He talked too much and had no brains, but was a very pleasant fellow. My mother could not bear him, and was always commenting on the fact that in the First War he appeared in khaki with *spurs*. He had been a volunteer in the Boer War, and though he had been too late to get to the front, he had the South African Medal. In the War he volunteered for home service and became a major, hence the spurs. Northcliffe picked a quarrel with him in 1909 because he said Percy had put some puffs in the *Mail* for medicines in which his agency was interested. In the following year he accused Percy of spreading greatly exaggerated reports of Northcliffe's ill-health. I think the quarrel was created out of nothing, or nearly nothing, by Northcliffe, who decided to ruin Percy by giving orders that none of his papers were to accept advertising from Percy's agency. Northcliffe didn't quite succeed, but he certainly did his best. On his death-bed he repented and told Christa he had been unjust. As a result, in the compromise will, Christa got twice the income received by the other two sisters. The cause of this quarrel seemed to me to stem from the fact that Northcliffe liked to be surrounded by men dependent on himself and was resentful that Percy had set up on his own account. With advancing years, Percy became increasingly exacting and difficult. His secretary (a very nice woman) eventually settled into the Burton household, to Christa's great relief. He left her such money as he possessed.

Vyvyan

The youngest of the family was Vyvyan, born when his mother was forty-seven. She married at the age of twenty-six and had fourteen children in twenty-one years. None of them, as she was proud to say, was a twin. She seemed to think twins were more like a litter, and therefore more becoming in a rabbit than a human being! He was always known as 'Boo', and was the most ordinary of all the eleven brothers and sisters. He was said to be the son most like his father in appearance, but to me he just seemed another Harmsworth with rather bucolic good looks. He was educated at Charterhouse and Cambridge, but achieved no academic or other distinction. He was simple, lazy and kind, and spent most of his time at Horstead Keynes in Sussex, where he did a little gentle farming. For a short time he was an apprentice in the *Evening News* machine room, but otherwise played no part in the business. Later in life he bought a small property at Thrumster, near Wick, in the far north of Scotland and shared his time between Caithness and Sussex. My mother was disgusted because once when she was at his house he lay on a sofa and called on his wife to pull off his riding-boots; he was too lazy to do it himself. Northcliffe upbraided him once for doing no work and he replied, 'What is the use of having a brother like you if I have to work?'

Fleet Street

During two long vacations, Northcliffe arranged for me to work in a newspaper office. The first time it was the *Daily Mail*, where I was in the news-room under Tom Clarke at the time of which he wrote in his book *My Northcliffe Diary*. The reporters with me were Prince White, Paul Bewsher and Montagu Smith, all well known in Fleet Street then and later. It was the end of the Northcliffe era. He made Glover, the huge commissionaire, advertisement director in top hat and tails – all a kind of sick joke. I am no reporter, and was far too shy to do well then. However, I got a paragraph in the main news page about a left-handed bowman in the statuary on the London County Hall. My most vivid recollection of these two months was when an elderly man with an umbrella came into the office and announced he was the first pregnant man. I was told off to keep him from going away by giving him tea, while those more experienced wrote up the story. However, the Charing Cross Hospital assured us that this was the commonest form of hallucination, so the tea was curtailed and he was ushered out.

The next long vacation I was attached to *The Times*, then under the editorship of Wickham Steed. He was a very foreign-looking man with a pointed beard, highly intelligent, but not, I imagine, a good editor. He had spent much of his life abroad, mostly in Vienna, and lived with a Jugoslav mistress. He looked at foreign affairs from a Middle European standpoint and knew little of the domestic affairs of this country. I did a little reporting, but the part I remember was sitting behind the editor's chair in the afternoon when the leaders were discussed for the following day's paper. It was at the time the Versailles Treaty was being negotiated and this confirmed my interest in politics, originally kindled by hearing my uncles talk politics in my grandmother's drawing-room.

I left Oxford in June 1922, when Northcliffe was already dying, so there was a period when I wondered whether he had given effect to his promises to leave me all the family heirlooms. As he had said I was his favourite nephew, it was at least possible some niche might be arranged for me at the *Daily Mail*. However, I was not mentioned in his various wills and eventually found the same as the other nephews. Northcliffe actually died in August and I then had to deal with Rothermere, an uncle I hardly knew. He owned the *Leeds Mercury* and the *Glasgow Record*, and was negotiating with the executors for the controlling interest in the *Daily Mail*. *The Times* was sold by the executors to John Astor and the Amalgamated Press to Lord Camrose. Rothermere sent me to Glasgow with my cousin Ronnie Harmsworth to learn how a newspaper ran. I was in Glasgow for nearly ten months and in that time spent periods in all the principal departments. I lived in a residential hotel, Moore's Hotel, and met Ronnie at breakfast. I had introductions to some of the wealthier citizens of Glasgow, with whom I had nothing in common, and also to some of the Ayrshire aristocracy, with whom I fared somewhat better. I was lonely, though engaged to be married. The newspapers, the *Glasgow Record* and *Sunday Mail*, were carefully run, but neither the editor, Campbell, nor the manager, Barr, ever explained to me what it was all about. I think the firm made the very large profit of £137,000 in the year I was there. Little trouble was taken with the editorial content, with the result, later on, that D. C. Thomson started the *Sunday Post*, which quickly pulled ahead of the *Sunday Mail*, where it has remained. Glasgow in 1922 was a raw, gloomy city to which I can have contributed nothing. In fact when out walking one day I was handed a tract *Through Crime to Christ*, so I must have looked pretty down and out!

It was in Glasgow that the first symptoms of psoriasis appeared, a disease which has acquired an ever greater hold over me as the years passed. It is a skin disease, believed to be the leprosy of the Old Testament, quite common, associated with good general health; its cause is quite unknown. It ebbs and flows, so sometimes for weeks on end it disappears, and at other times it can be acutely painful for days at a time, or violently irritating for months. For most of my adult life it has been like wearing a painfully uncomfortable hair shirt. It was due to this that I was rejected D4 by a medical board at Reading during the Second War. D4 means you are unsuitable for any kind of military service.

After nine-and-a-half months in Glasgow I persuaded Rothermere to let me come south and join the staff of the *Daily Mail*. At first I had a spell with the auditors, which gave me a view of the business from the financial end, and later I moved to the Ideas and Business Development department under G. H. Grimaldi.

When I joined the staff Northcliffe had only been dead a year. Though he had been away and later desperately ill for the two years before his death, he was the only man who could make serious decisions. Tom Marlowe, at £34,000 per annum, was the titular editor, but the active editor-in-chief was Northcliffe. The managing director of Associated Newspapers was Andrew Caird, also at £34,000 per annum. But here, too, all serious decisions, on finance, on labour matters and on advertising were taken by Northcliffe in his life-time. At his death these titles became realities and for the first time the incumbents were called upon to perform. Caird was a mean, penny-pinching Scotsman. This is always dangerous in a newspaper – in cutting out extravagance it is so easy to cut the heart out of a paper. Marlowe seemed to me a dignified nonentity. I remember hearing he had had a reporter up and ticked him off for some low-life story, saying, 'Don't forget, my boy, the

Daily Mail is read in Park Lane.' Northcliffe's version was that the paper should be edited as if its readers all had a thousand a year (a lot of money in those days). But whereas Northcliffe's dictum really amounted to editing somewhat above the heads of the readers, Marlowe's was snobbery pure and simple, and of no help to a popular paper. What impressed me deeply at the time was that the whole *Daily Mail* group depended on one man. There was no management structure, and when the one man died the business quickly suffered. The part that survived best was the news-getting side. The *Daily Mail* continued to get stories the other papers would have given their eye-teeth for and this for at least twenty years. The contrast in this respect was with W. H. Smith, an organization which went on its way unperturbed by the death of St John Hornby, to whom so much of the present enterprise is due.

Of all the people I have encountered in my business life, George Grimaldi was one of the ablest. He taught me how to write a business letter: 'Always begin with "you", never with "I".' The department he headed was the Promotion department in fact, though called Ideas and Business Development. He suffered from bad health and died at a fairly early age, but the main reason for his relative lack of success seemed to me to be a lack of an adequate sense of direction. The head of the Advertising department, and hence Grimaldi's boss, was C. Stephen Millikin, a forceful and able man, who had served a term of imprisonment. He had advertised cheap shirts, collected the money but not delivered the shirts. This episode in his past was apparently unknown to his employers and he ended up many years later as a director of Associated Newspapers.

Rothermere never came to the office and knew none of the staff, but ran the company, in so far as he did so at all, by summoning Caird or Marlowe, mostly Caird, to his flat in the Savoy Hotel. He was interested primarily in the politics of the *Daily Mail* and secondarily in the price of Associated Newspaper shares. He must have been a superlatively able Wall Street spectacular but in the more human business of running a newspaper, he seemed to me to be without aptitude of any kind. In general, he preferred to deal with the inferior, such as the man who doubled the job of procurer with a directorship of the *Sunday Pictorial*. His ablest lieutenant, Bertrand Lima, died of Spanish 'flu in 1919 when he was in his middle thirties. Otherwise I cannot recall any particular talent in his entourage.

In 1926, after three years in the *Daily Mail*, I was made a director of the Empire Paper Mills and I was given a trip round the Mediterranean to Lisbon, Madeira, Cadiz, Athens and Constantinople. On my return I was told I was transferred to the *Daily Mirror*. At that time Rothermere had about eighty per cent of the voting shares in the *Mirror*, which controlled the Sunday Pictorial Company, and the Daily Mirror and Sunday Pictorial Companies jointly controlled the Daily Mail Trust, which controlled Associated Newspapers, which in turn controlled the Anglo-Newfoundland Development Co. The paper itself was originally a picture paper at a time when the other newspapers published few pictures. It had had the biggest sale in the world in 1917 but by the time I came on the scene it had fallen back and the *Daily Mail* was easily in the lead. It had been bought from Northcliffe in 1913 or 1914 at a time when Rothermere severed his connection with the Associated Newspapers. Rothermere's first move on assuming control was to fire all the circulation travellers as a measure of economy. One of those fired was Freddie Poke, easily the ablest man ever employed by the Harmsworth brothers.

I had been told to see John Cowley at the *Mirror* office in Bouverie Street and find out what I was to do. I remember having a talk with Cowley when someone came into the room. Cowley said, 'I am just running the ruler over this young man.' I remember thinking at the time that Cowley's assessment of my gifts or abilities would be of little value.

John Cowley was then, and for nearly twenty years longer, chairman of the Daily Mirror and Sunday Pictorial Companies. He had been the cashier of the *Evening News* at a pound a week when that newspaper was bought by the Harmsworths in 1894.

He had subsequently become general manager of the *Daily Mail*, and his name is in the imprint of the first issue. He subsequently quarrelled with Northcliffe about the year 1908, and put his savings into a new evening paper with Bernard Falk and Edgar Wallace. This failed and he started a trade paper for newsagents. This may have survived, but he dropped out and was in very straitened circumstances when Rothermere found him during the War and made him secretary of the Anglo-Newfoundland Company. When Lima died in 1919, Cowley was appointed chairman of the Mirror and Pictorial Companies, where he remained until he died in 1944. John Cowley, who is said to have had Isaac as a second christian name, was a man without ability that I could ever discern. He was rather above medium height, with good features and a rather distinguished appearance. His value to Rothermere was that he would do exactly what Rothermere told him to do, however foolish or dishonest. Inside the office, restoring the fallen fortunes of the *Daily Mirror* was problem enough, but to achieve success in spite of the constant obstruction of the chairman, the general manager and the finance director was quite something. Until about 1935 Cowley represented the controlling shareholder. He had no initiative of his own and simply sat there to see that Rothermere's wishes were carried out. After 1935 Rothermere had sold his shares on the market and Cowley remained on, alarmed at the circulation, which had declined, but almost more alarmed by our efforts to rehabilitate the paper. In all the years I knew Cowley I can only recall one good remark of his. He told me that I should remember that when he came into Fleet Street the leading evening paper was the *Echo* – now dead: the leading Sunday paper was *Lloyd's Sunday News* – now dead: and the leading daily paper was the *Standard* – now dead.

He was another secretive type. When he lay dying, efforts were made to get in touch with his relatives. But neither his secretary of twenty-four years standing nor his three sons could throw any light on his ancestry or his family connections. He was believed to have had a brother who may have been a Fleet Street hairdresser, and he is thought to have had sisters whom he supported financially. His sons said he seemed to know the Holloway district very well indeed, so he may have been born or brought up there. I knew him for eighteen years and had never heard him give any information at all on his origins. Like the Harmsworths he was desperately anxious to conceal his humble beginning, of which he might reasonably have been proud.

For my first three years I was assistant advertisement manager under one Willmott. Then, by much importuning, I got Rothermere to make me a director of the Mirror Company, and with it I became advertisement director, which I nominally remained for ten years or more.

When I joined the *Mirror*, it was run essentially by three men, Cowley, whom I have already mentioned, Wally Roome the general manager, and Jimmy Lovell the finance director. The chairman saw that Rothermere's wishes were carried out. Wally Roome had a good deal of superficial charm and was very quick and shrewd where his personal interests were involved, but contributed nothing to the Company. Jimmy Lovell was a nicer man, and conceived it to be his duty to mind the bawbees. This he did in a very unimaginative way that strangled any new development. No money was ever to be spent on anything new. Though I was the advertisement director, I was not allowed any expenses either for travel (e.g. to Manchester) or for entertaining. The only other director of any consequence was Bartholomew, who had been appointed in Northcliffe's day. Of him more later. Both at the *Daily Mail* and at the *Mirror* for a total of quite fifteen years every effort was made to freeze me out. A public school and university education was no help in the wilder shores of Fleet Street. I was given no executive responsibility until I was thirty-three and, even then, anything I achieved was by subterfuge. When I became a director of the Company I was not allowed to see any of the firm's figures, though I knew we were doing very badly. So I told the secretary of the Company I would get an injunction compelling Cowley to let me see what was happening. However, Bill Jennings, the secretary said he would show me any figures I wished to see, and Cowley would not know. This was obviously a more amicable way of gaining my objective and was quite satisfactory to me. Since then the firm has got inside a number of companies as a result of take-over bids only to discover that sometimes the directors were kept in the dark by the chairman or managing director. Such a situation is evidently quite common in British industry.

After I had been advertisement director for some time, it was evident that I could not hope to sell advertising in a newspaper which was vaguely supposed to be doing about a million, but was in fact slipping at the rate of 70,000 a year and by 1933 was under 800,000. I was allowed no good staff and no expenses, which would have made selling space an uphill struggle anyway. However, the most important thing was to get the sale moving up. Drifting around the office, a director of long standing but with no real job, was Guy Bartholomew. He had ideas, I had good judgement, so we put our heads together. The editor at that time was one L. D. Brownlee, who should have been sporting editor of *The Times*. He was very knowledgeable about cricket, but was quite the wrong man to produce a popular paper. To get any of our ideas across, Brownlee had to be removed. In the end, favoured by the catastrophic sales figures, Brownlee was paid off, but Cowley would not have Bartholomew as editor, probably rightly, and Cecil Thomas was appointed. He could be relied on to be receptive to our ideas and his rotund, rather bucolic appearance was reassuring for the ever-fearful Cowley.

The *Mirror* had been founded, after an initial false start, as a picture paper to be bought with one of the others. But in the depressed conditions of the early thirties, people found they could do without the second, the picture paper, as the text papers by that time had as many pictures as the *Mirror*. In

1919 Col. McCormick and Captain Paterson had been to see Northcliffe at Elmwood and had asked his advice on the launching of a paper in New York. He advised them to produce a Daily Mirror, which they did, and the resulting *Daily News* is a success to this day. But the *Daily News* was not meant as a second, picture paper, but as a paper with pictures which would attract the less educated who, at that time, did not perhaps buy a daily paper at all. So in 1933 we thought it might be wise to seek inspiration from the *Daily News*. We also thought the American advertising agencies with their copy in strip form had lessons to teach us. At that time there were no strip cartoons in the English papers, though Haselden for years had drawn something similar for the *Mirror*. His cartoons were square, and the appeal of a strip cartoon is that it reads compellingly from left to right. This is no doubt why the rise of television has seen the decline of the strip cartoon.

As I have always been interested in politics, I took over the political guidance of the new-style *Daily Mirror*. As a companion paper its politics had been rather wishy-washy but extreme right wing. If we were to move the *Mirror* into a new market, it would have to be the working-class market. Each paper that has reached the top sale has done so by appealing to a class which did not previously read a daily paper. So *The Times* was followed successively by the *Telegraph*, the *Daily Mail*, and the *Express*. Our best hope was therefore to appeal to young working-class men and women, and in general the least educated part of the population. If this was the aim, the politics had to be made to match. In the depression of the thirties there was no future in preaching right wing politics to young people in the lowest income bracket. In any case my own instinctive sympathies have been for the under-dog, and certainly at that time included a strong sympathy with the aspirations of women, who were treated in so many ways as second-class citizens. The criterion I used to apply was to ask of a paragraph if it was of interest to, or intelligible by, a bus driver's wife in Sheffield. If not, then it should not have been printed. This criterion excludes a certain amount but, more important, imposes on a great deal more a high standard of simple clear English. The changes in the *Mirror* horrified my uncles, who did not wish to be reminded of their origins in the popular newspaper world. Had not the *Daily Mail* in its early days been described as the 'van-boys' own', 'edited by office-boys for office-boys'? But by the thirties, with their fortunes and their titles, they had no wish to be reminded of events forty years earlier. Rothermere reluctantly made me a director of the Sunday Pictorial Company in 1935, after he had publicly announced that he had severed his connection with Geraldine House.

Cowley did at one time tell me that there was not room for both of us in the building. Either he would have to go, or I should. I said I had no intention of leaving and heard no more about it!

I think the most surprising thing about the new *Mirror* was the speed of public response. On the first day Bart took over he put two pictures of an American lynching quite small on the front page, and for the first time for a very long while the sale went up, and kept on up. The trouble we ran into with the advertisers was that they didn't like a tabloid paper, and we were bound to lose some advertising before a strongly rising sale got us into the big time. However, we had the support of J. Walter Thompson's and also of Unilever, and passed through a difficult period with less difficulty than we might have expected.

I feel that, at this point, I should attempt a picture of 'Bart', as we all knew him. He was one of two brothers, the sons of a Mrs Bartholomew, who was represented to me as a great character. Bart was short and square, very good-looking, with a shock of white hair, and with features and mannerisms not unlike Northcliffe, whose illegitimate son he was quite erroneously supposed to have been. Roome used to tell the story of Mrs Bartholomew sending an SOS to Guy to rescue Claud, who was entangled with an undesirable girl in Glasgow. He returned married to her! Bertha Bartholomew was a vulgar old thing who kept Guy firmly under her thumb. She had been married before and had had a daughter, who died. She and Bart adopted a son, Peter, who, when I last heard of him, was manager of the Cardiff commercial television operation. Bertha did not want it known that Peter was adopted, nor that she was seven years older than her husband. After her death her family discovered that in fact she had been thirteen years older than Guy! The difficulty in giving any facts about Bart's early days lies in his capacity for romance. However, he clearly had had very little schooling, and appeared at the *Daily Mirror* in its earliest days as manager of the process engraving dept. He claimed to be a Jew, which was untrue; that he was brought up in a charity school (I doubt this); that he was related to General Bartholomew (perhaps); that his grandfather drove a cab in Horsham – but there was no mention of his father.

By the time I knew him he was full of energy, almost wholly frustrated. He had taken photographs on the battle-field in the First War and had played a part in inventing the Bart-Lane process for picture transmission. He was a good photographer, a brilliant picture editor, had a great understanding of strip cartoons and, lastly, he was full of ideas, most of them bad. My rôle at that stage was to plan the campaign to get rid of Brownlee and to filter the good ideas from the bad, keeping the good ones constantly to the fore until they were executed.

Bart was nearly illiterate. On one or two occasions I had letters from him written when there was no secretary at hand. These letters were quite illiterate – sentences did not end or had no verbs. He had an acute sense of educational inferiority, and his attitude to me was a mixture of envy and resentment of my background plus a recognition of my ability. He once said to me, 'You are not liked but you are respected. You are bloody hard, but you are just.' This did not prevent his trying to injure me when opportunity offered.

Hulton decided to start a Sunday edition of the *Daily Sketch* in 1915. Much publicity was devoted to the new venture, of which fairly long notice was given. Rothermere hit on the idea of bringing out a Sunday edition of the *Daily Mirror* the week before. So was born the *Sunday Pictorial*, which got away to a flying start and was never nearly overtaken by Hulton's rival. The new paper was naturally got together in a hurry by the *Mirror* staff. When two issues had been published and the paper was a success, the *Mirror* staff were sent back to the *Mirror* while a team arrived from the *Glasgow Record* to take over the new paper. Bart had played a part in all this but was never given any shares (as were others) nor any recognition of any kind. The result was a life-long vendetta against the *Sunday Pictorial*. Even when, in the fullness of time, he became chairman of the Sunday Pictorial Company, he still did all he could to injure the newspaper!

When Cowley died, I suppose I was the obvious successor, but we had brought back John Coope from Northcliffe Newspapers. Bart was the senior director and had done more than anyone else at that stage to resuscitate the paper. I told Bart he would make a very bad chairman, but if that was the reward he wanted for his services, he would have my vote. Bart professed not to want the job. I knew this was nonsense, but I did not know that he was involved in a complicated intrigue with Jimmy Lovell and John Coope, with the result that Bart became chairman of both companies: John Coope became vice-chairman of the *Mirror*, with a promise of the succession, and I was made vice-chairman of the *Sunday Pictorial*. Bart did indeed prove to be a bad chairman. John Coope soon showed his inadequacy, and after twelve months Bart had written Coope off, and I was back in his fickle favour. Roome had died before Cowley, and so had not been involved in all this. Though Bart was amusing and at times brilliant, he was a dreadful man to work with or for. He enjoyed spying on people, and so our telephones were tapped and our letters read. Any critical remark about any member of the staff would be passed on by Bart to create mischief. If no critical remark was made he would often concoct one. Setting different members of the staff – or the board – at each other's throats was a real pleasure for him. This, of course, is the reverse of the proper rôle of a chairman. Towards the end of his reign I got more and more involved in our West African papers, and Bart's spirit and influence became more and more perceptible in the paper. Eventually his drunkenness reached such proportions that something had to be done. He had got to the point of insulting distinguished guests at lunch, repeatedly alleging, for instance, to the head of the Australian Radio Control Board, Sir Lionel Hook, that 'all Australians were crooks', mercifully said so incoherently as to be nearly unintelligible. Eventually I collected the votes of my colleagues, who said I would never succeed in shifting Bart, but that I had their vote. Then early one morning (he was usually incoherent by 9.30 a.m.) I told him he had lost the confidence of his board and must vacate the chair. He rang one of the other directors, Bolam, the editor, and found he was supporting me, so his reign was over. He lingered on that morning, weeping maudlin tears into his whisky in the company of the hall porter.

Of course, when starting out to create a new kind of newspaper, I had no real idea where I should end up – certainly not with a total sale of *Mirror* and *Glasgow Record* verging on six million a day. One point we had clearly in view, that the paper had to be edited on the assumption that our readers listened in to the BBC news every morning, and that therefore any attempt to get news scoops was a waste of effort. Though broadcasting had then been in existence for over ten years, the papers were, in the main, edited as if the BBC did not exist. This is sometimes still true. People come out with what was once a truism but is now not true, that a newspaper 'exists to give the news'. Another aspect of the same thing was to realize that a popular newspaper is in part in the entertainment business. People buy the *Mirror*, not for the day's news, but to be entertained on their way to work and at lunch. Maybe you can insert in the sugar coating a pill of news and views you think they should read. But that is not what the paper is basically for.

Another simple discovery of that period is that half the

human race is female. The result is to realize that women must not only be catered for in the feature pages but in the news columns as well. Women in general are not interested in politics, business or sport, but are interested in people. So to gain a female readership, and these are the people the advertisers want, your news columns must have plenty of human interest stories. They may be trivial, but they have an emotional impact and this interests everybody, and particularly women. Bartholomew not only took no interest in sport, he would not allow any proper coverage in the *Daily Mirror* while he was an active member of the board. It was a great feat forcing up the sale of the paper in spite of a derisory coverage of sport, which is the great daily subject of entertainment among men.

What caused the rumpus was our attitude to sex. The prevailing attitude at that time was that sex was a nasty secret. The *News of the World*, which sold on sex and sport, regarded sex as something the butler saw through the key-hole. I think we were the first newspaper to deal frankly with the subject of birth-control and to publish pictures of curvaceous ladies in bathing dresses. Nothing we did then would cause the slightest stir now, but at the time it was a risky life, as John Cowley had no idea what was going on and had to be pacified with constant reassurances that it was all 'in good taste'. It was supposed by our competitors that we should assemble a small readership of adolescent boys before we went broke. My uncles warned me I should end in gaol, but I didn't think then that we were running any risks except from our elders in the office, and one can see now that we were playing dead safe.

The curious part about the rise of the *Daily Mirror* is that it has always been ignored by the other popular newspapers. Long after we had declared ourselves as *the* danger to the *Express*, the *Express* was ignoring us and concentrating on the *Daily Mail*. Even now, Fleet Street tends to regard the *Mirror* as beneath its notice. This has been a great help, as with all-out competition in the early stages, we would have been in trouble. Quite recently Tom Blackburn of the *Express* complained at a meeting of the Newspaper Proprietors' Association that the *Mirror* was 'a phenomenon, not a newspaper'. One fact that emerged in the early days was that women like pictures of bathing belles as much as men, though for different reasons. It was many years before our competitors got around to that one.

We had, of course, no useful contacts of any description. In so far as the paper had anything of the kind, it depended on Rothermere. When he withdrew, he left nothing behind. This was brought home to us in a very marked form at the time of the Abdication. The people behind the *Mail*, the *Express* and *The Times* were all actively involved, while we were dependent on what came in from the agencies. Cudlipp and I vowed at that time never to be caught in the dark by some crisis like this ever again. As a result, over the years, we have acquired better sources of information over the whole field, political, diplomatic, financial, scientific, etc., than any other paper. This is not difficult, but it costs some money in lunches and so forth, and it does require assiduity over a long period, and it is this element that the other papers tend to fall short on.

But to get back to the earliest days of the new *Mirror*. The problem was to find some bright editorial sparks to make the paper attractive to the young. Bill Connor, then writing copy for the Harpic account, and Basil Nicholson, then writing copy for the Horlicks account, had been to see me with some strip cartoons they had been working on. I don't remember whether we made use of their cartoons, but we certainly accepted the importance of strip cartoons to a popular paper at that time, and Popeye and Jane became household names throughout the country and for many years. But as a result of my meeting these two, we took them on the staff, Connor to end thirty-odd years later as Sir William Connor and still writing for us under the *nom de plume* Cassandra. Basil Nicholson remained for some years, went back to the agency world, returned to us but left again, and finally died miserably of cancer of the throat in Dublin. We did our best to ease his death-bed, but for years his heavy drinking had made it impossible for him to keep down a steady job. He was certainly among the half-dozen most brilliant men I ever met. He threw off ideas like a catherine wheel. Many of them were quite unusable, but perhaps that was where I came in, sifting the wheat from the chaff. He wrote a book called *Business is Business*, which has enough bright ideas to last a successful novelist a lifetime. But so many ideas in such a small compass make the book almost unreadable.

In an attempt to get some brighter staff we advertised for a features editor. Among the replies, I can still remember opening a letter from Hugh Cudlipp, then working on the *Sunday Chronicle* in London under James Drawbell. Cudlipp had answered the advertisement for a lark. He was twenty-one but had had by then seven years' experience of journalism in South Wales and in Lancashire. He was hired, and it was really the triumvirate of Bartholomew, Nicholson and Cudlipp who created the new *Mirror*, while I supplied the ballast, the sense of direction and continuity which were very necessary. Cudlipp at that time had little education, no foresight, but a galaxy of journalistic gifts. He was a brilliant reporter and sub-editor: he had acquired a wonderful technique for lay-out from Drawbell, and has a gift for timing which is quite beyond price in a daily paper. Over the years he has acquired an excellent education, and has picked up from me a habit of looking ahead which, once acquired, cannot be forgotten. I have always felt that chess should be a part of every business executive's training. It is not necessary to be a good chess player, but even bumble-puppy chess forces one to consider the immediate consequences of any move one may make.

But to return to Hugh Cudlipp. Though there were no journalists in the family, the eldest brother Percy was the first to reach an editorship – that of the *Evening Standard*, and Reg was the last – that of the *News of the World*. But Hugh was the youngest and by far the ablest. In the popular paper field in my time, Hugh Cudlipp has been the outstanding editor anywhere in the world. In the more serious press you have figures like Beuve-Méry of *Le Monde*, with whom it is not possible to make a comparison. But the outstanding popular newspaper editors of my time might be Hearst, Beaverbrook and Springer, and the *Mirror* has certainly been a better and more successful popular paper than any put out by the three men I have named. It was, of course, an achievement of partners, but the man who put the words on the page throughout was Hugh Cudlipp.

After the new *Mirror* was clearly a success, the next step was obviously to re-vamp the *Sunday Pictorial* on the same lines. It had lost a million sale in ten years and was clearly heading for disaster. The idea was put forward that we should put ideas to the editor and that he would incorporate them in the paper. This never works. In the end the editor says your ideas are no good - look at the sale - and you complain that his interpretation has ruined your good ideas. However, in the end the editor departed, and we met twice in Cowley's room to make Bart editor of the *Sunday Pictorial*. Each time Bart was so rude to Cowley that he refused to make the appointment. However, I had recently been made a director of the Sunday Pictorial Company and eventually I was made editorial director. Bart said I could have any of the *Mirror* men as my editor (this was very typical of Bart), he had interviewed any possible editors and told them that if they accepted any offer from me he would do his best to ruin them. However, I invited Hugh Cudlipp to be editor and he accepted. He was twenty-four. This infuriated Bart, who kept us out of the *Mirror* as far as possible, and was obstructive in every way. What annoyed him more than anything was that the *Pictorial* sale soon started going up, and for many years kept 200,000 in front of the *Mirror*. This was infuriating (*a*) because the *Mirror* was his paper, (*b*) because he hated the *Pictorial* anyway, but (*c*) because the continued success of the *Pictorial* underlined the fact that he was neither entirely indispensable on the *Mirror*, nor was he wholly responsible for its success.

The change on the *Pictorial* took place in 1937 and meant, as it had on the *Mirror*, a change from right wing politics to support of the Labour Party. Bart from then on barred me from the *Mirror* as much as he could, so that my political influence, anti-Hitler, anti-Mussolini, anti-Franco, was more visible in the *Pictorial* than the *Mirror*, and thus it was in the *Pictorial* in 1939 that we started the year with 'Be Ready by Spring', and later urged the inclusion of Churchill in the Government and, still later, that he should take over as PM.

I was always in a sort of love-hate relationship with Bart. However much he resented my background, he appreciated my ability. So I was deputed in 1939 to be the link between the *Mirror* and Churchill when for a time he contributed a weekly article. He had been writing for the *News Chronicle*, but when they dropped him, we took him on. At that time he was very worried about German rearmament, and had a good deal of private information which cut across any figures given by the Government in public. For I suppose about two years I saw a good deal of Churchill, more at the beginning and less at the end. The eulogies of him have always seemed to me wildly exaggerated. He was an attractive personality with a good command of English, either written or spoken. He spent a lot of money and was not proud or fastidious in the ways he acquired what he spent, pot-boilers for the *News of the World* or financial subsidies from Beaverbrook and Rothermere. He had, very surprisingly, a very strong educational inferiority complex. He was very self-conscious about not having been to a university. As a politician he was not the equal of Lloyd George, and in the War was really Commander-in-Chief. There was no Prime Minister. Commentators who make the point that in the Second War there were no squabbles between the generals and the politicians miss the point. The generalissimo was in No. 10. The disastrous errors made at the end of the War were mainly Roosevelt's, but Churchill played a considerable part, too. As a man he was more self-centred than anyone I ever met. Any personal relationship had to begin with appreciation and flattery by the other man. If Churchill didn't like him, that was not enough, but it was the only means of attaining recognition. When we saw Lloyd George early in the War, he said to Cudlipp and myself, 'I see you are booming Churchill for Prime Minister. He won't be good: he will appoint only his friends and they are the wrong people.' And so it was. During the War Churchill surrounded himself with his friends, so many of whom were men of no calibre. He always seemed to me to be at heart a gifted adventurer. Politics were a glamorous career for him. Service to his country was a subject for rhetoric. What he looked for in other men was service to himself. The adventurer in him responded to Beaverbrook and Birkenhead, fellow-buccaneers. Early in the War he regarded the conflict as a personal one between Hitler and himself. This alarmed me, as between Hitler and Churchill, if one thought in those terms, Churchill was a non-starter. Later on, criticism of the Government was treason, even if one was only repeating what he had said about his fellow Ministers when they were in Chamberlain's Cabinet and he was out of office.

I remember a lunch at 10 Downing Street. I think the only other guest was Brendan Bracken. There had been an air raid the night before and reports of a particularly large bomb. I asked if this would have been a nuclear bomb. I didn't put it like that, and no one took me up on it, so I suppose they didn't understand what I meant. I never understood all the mystery about it at the end of the War. Sir George Thomson had been to stay with us at my then home, Culham Court, in 1939, before the war started, and in talking about recent scientific advances in his field, told me about the discovery of nuclear fission and how, at any rate in principle, it could be developed into a super-bomb if you could get together a critical amount of uranium 235. It was never put to me there was any secret about it. Nor really was there. The secret was the technique by which the uranium 235 could be separated from the 238. In fact I can well see that the technology was top secret, but the idea must have been known to anyone working in nuclear physics. The idea was, anyway, partly French, worked out by Madame Curie and her husband. Fermi, an Italian, also played a leading part.

111

My father was not financially minded, and at home no conversation of a financial nature took place. When I took over the management of the family money in 1926, I started with the idea that inflation was to be guarded against, and so investment should be in equities. In fact I never invested any money in gilt-edged, and only occasionally in preference shares when they were quoted at such a discount as to partake of the character of an ordinary share with recovery prospects.

However, in 1937 I was sent to Canada to straighten out the capital structure of the Anglo-Canadian Pulp & Paper Company. It had been founded in 1926 to develop the Manicouagan timber limits on the north shore of the St Lawrence, about three hundred miles down-stream from Quebec. This ill-conceived venture was part of Rothermere's obsession that the supply of timber for newsprint was nearly exhausted, and so the whole of the newspaper industry was under constant threat. It was this obsession of Rothermere's that had persuaded Northcliffe to found the Anglo-Newfoundland Development Company's mill at Grand Falls in 1905. That led to the disastrous purchase of Gulf Pulp & Paper for $5,000,000 in 1920, and that finally led to the establishment of the Anglo-Canadian Co. in 1926. These Manicouagan limits were in fact unworkable and have never been worked. When the mill was half up, this was suddenly realized and there was a last minute rush to find timber limits for wood on which the mill would operate. The Oxford Paper Company had some limits on the Montmorency near Quebec. They had cut out the best timber and the balsam fir that was left was thought to have such a low density and such a high dirt count as not to be worth having. However, any port in a storm, and the Montmorency limits were bought, partly for cash and partly for shares. The Anglo-Canadian mill had four machines, and no study had been made on the wisdom of adding the output of four machines to the market, plus other machines simultaneously going up at Reed's. They contributed to a surplus of newsprint production and, in any case, the whole industry was overtaken by the slump of 1929. By 1937 the time had come, I thought, for simplifying the capital structure of the Anglo-Canadian Company, which by then was a hodge-podge of loans, debentures, preference shares in arrears, and more or less worthless common shares which had originally been pure water. I persuaded Rothermere, and subsequently Cowley and Roome that the matter should be tackled, and off I went having no financial experience for this kind of work. First I had to buy a block of preference shares from Chisholm, president of the Oxford Paper Company. I was authorized to pay £80,000 and did my utmost to get them for £40,000, but eventually had to pay £45,000, for which no one ever said thank you! However, the capital reconstruction was approved and was really very satisfactory. My directorship of the Empire Paper Mills for some years from 1926 and my interest in the Anglo-Canadian Company from 1937 onwards gave me a working knowledge of the paper trade, which was useful to me later.

One episode of the immediate pre-war period sticks in my memory. We were friends with Walton Butterworth, I think through his wife. He was at that time second man at the American Embassy and, subsequently, American Ambassador in Canada. Through him I was asked to dinner in 1938 by the Ambassador, Joe Kennedy. One of the other guests was Beaverbrook, whom I had never met before. As he shook hands with me he said, 'Well, young man, you have made your mark in Fleet Street.' I was very surprised as I did not see myself in that light, and it was many years before such an idea was widely held. I never saw much of Beaverbrook, perhaps a dozen times in all, once alone in his flat in Arlington Street; twice at big lunches for visiting celebrities, once at dinner with Ben Smith (the Wolf of Wall Street) in New York.

I have been wondering where my interest in politics started. I think it was listening to my uncles talking politics in my grandmother's drawing-room when I was a youth. Then my spell at *The Times* contributed a further interest – in foreign affairs this time. I had three relations in the House of Commons in the twenties – Cecil Harmsworth was Liberal MP for Droitwich and subsequently Luton, Leicester Harmsworth was Liberal MP for Caithness and Sutherland, and Esmond Harmsworth was Conservative MP for the Isle of Thanet. I suppose I might have had one of these seats, but it never occurred to me to try. The practical objections were that I had no money and was too shy to be good in debate. But the main reason was my uncle's experience. Northcliffe had indeed fought an election at Portsmouth, but saw very early on that it is far pleasanter to play a political rôle from a newspaper office than from the benches of the House of Commons. I have never seen any reason to disagree with this view. I was startled when talking to Churchill in 1939 when he said everyone interested in politics was in the House of Commons. If they were not there, it was because they had tried to get in and failed. Not only did I think such an idea nonsense, I had never heard it put forward before.

It became clear to me early in 1939 that war was inevitable, and I considered my own position. It was obvious that at my age (thirty-eight) I was unlikely to be able to play any military part, and in fact I was later rejected on health grounds and graded D4. It was well known that our armaments were inadequate for us to wage any aggressive war for a long time. But in the First War the Germans had shown far more fear of Northcliffe and his propaganda than they did of our military efforts. In any case, in England in 1939 we had nearly all the good advertising and publicity people outside North America. Propaganda only required the skilled people we had, some offices and typewriters and we were in business. Most of the advertising people might be unwelcome in Whitehall, but I had the same social and educational background as the senior civil servants, and I had spent fifteen years on the borderline between journalism and advertising. Surely I was just what was wanted! So I made enquiries and found that in the event of war Sam Hoare was to be the Minister in charge of the Ministry of Information and the Public Trustee at the time was to be the Permanent Under-Secretary. It was agreed that the Censor should be an admiral. This lunatic set-up was just the first form the organization took. It was subject to frequent changes, but one principle was immutable: no one at the MOI must know anything about propaganda, popular opinion, mass communications, or anything of the kind. The Censor should, of course, have been a civilian to whom the military chiefs would have had to make a case if they wanted anything suppressed. The outcome, as one might have expected, was that censorship was used quite cynically to keep from the British public news that was well known to the enemy, but which might have reflected discredit on ministers, generals or admirals. And the Ministry of Information was cluttered up with museum staff who not only knew nothing of wartime propaganda, but were temperamentally unsuited to that kind of work.

I applied for a job some months before the War began – a job in the embryo MOI. I was seen by a rather dim and junior civil servant who explained the pay would be much less than what I was getting, not more than twelve hundred a year, which would be a big drop. I said it would be war work, so that was all right. The little man said he would let me know shortly how my application had fared. I never received an acknowledgement, let alone acceptance or rejection. This was the first of four applications, to none of which did I get a reply of any kind!

I once asked why we had no effective propaganda department in the Second War, though it had obviously been effective in the First War and was something Hitler was clearly afraid of. It was put to me by someone whose name I have forgotten but who might know. He said that to spread effective propaganda you must have a policy. It is like selling a commercial commodity. If you can't decide whether your product is tea or whisky, you obviously can't set about selling it. Churchill had no policy. He looked on the War as a sort of football match. If we got more goals than the Germans we should have won and could go home. Churchill resented any talk of propaganda, as any effort in that direction would have required a clear statement of policy, which was in fact non-existent.

Though introducing museum personnel into the MOI may seem eccentric, this was in fact part of a regular policy. Clearly, in wartime you want more administrators in Government service, so one would have thought you would recruit the best of the business chiefs. But not so, Leathers was brought in because he was a personal friend of Churchill, and Woolton was in fact PRO at the Ministry of Food while Henry French ran the show. But hordes of university dons were recruited, who knew nothing of administration but had the same sort of academic record as the administrative class civil servants. So they talked the same language, and were not likely to be troublesome, as they knew even less about administration than the civil servants.

Trying to recall the state of mind at the outbreak of war, I remember my own feelings were strongly influenced by a talk I had with 'Squeaker' Curtis, then Deputy-Commandant of the Staff College. He had been a subaltern in the King's Royal Rifles with my brother. He explained that the Germans were planning to spray our cities with mustard gas from the air. As the 'gas' is in fact a heavy oily substance, it can be broken up into a fine spray, which will slowly and invisibly float to earth. If this falls on the eyes, the result is blindness. Hence, at any rate, part of the reason for the insistence by the authorities on the carrying of gas masks everywhere. The result was that gasmasks, which proved entirely unnecessary, were one of the very few actual preparations for the war. Another was said to be millions of cardboard coffins for the huge death-roll expected in the cities. Had the death-roll been as high as had been feared, I doubt whether recourse would have been had to the cardboard coffins. Another aspect of the same misjudgement was the widespread evacuation of children from the cities. A horde of Glaswegian Catholics, women and children, descended on my parish of Cushnie in Aberdeenshire. When they ascertained that the nearest pub was four and a half miles away and the nearest priest seven miles, they gave up and went home, not before horrifying the very thrifty Aberdonians by sitting on the steps of the Post Office and smoking away their dole money.

The policy of the *Daily Mirror* in the late thirties, and still more that of the *Sunday Pictorial*, with which I was more immediately concerned, had been to warn its readers of the danger of war, the menace of the dictators, Hitler and Mussolini, and the wisdom of listening to Churchill's warnings. So much was this so that I am told the directors of the *Daily Mirror* were among those to be arrested immediately on the occupation of London by the German forces. It was a disappointment to find, when Churchill finally took office in 1940, that what was wrong with pre-war governments, in Churchill's eyes, was not so much that their policy was wrong, but that he was not in office. Once in office he was very happy to have the support of those politicians whose inadequacies he had unsparingly denounced before the War. The *Daily Telegraph* had been anti-Churchill, but once Churchill was in office Camrose, its proprietor, became *persona grata*, whereas Churchill did his best to suppress the *Daily Mirror*, which had been his friend when he had few others. The general line pursued by our papers was for a more vigorous prosecution of the War, the promotion of younger men and the removal of those politicians whose activities throughout the thirties had been so ruinous for the country.

As my medical examination classified me as D4, there was no kind of work left available to me. I was therefore a spectator of events, a recipient of the gossip in Fleet Street and Whitehall. Of this I kept a diary from January 1940 till the end of hostilities. I was still editorial director of the *Sunday Pictorial* and so spent every Saturday night in the office. If there was an air raid, I stayed until the all-clear, in this way coming in for the biggest raid of the War. As I had never been in any physical danger before, I was interested to see what would happen when I was in the middle of a really bad raid. I am very nervous in any aeroplane, where the danger is minimal, but in an air raid I was not frightened. It was interesting to see the reactions of the staff, most of them being splendidly courageous, which made the behaviour of the cowards all the more conspicuous. Our sub-editors were magnificent, working under a glass roof; so were the van-drivers going through the blitz on unlighted roads, often full of bomb craters and covered with debris. I rode with them occasionally: they did it nearly every night.

I remember we had an enquiry from a reader who asked why his fish and chips was always wrapped up in the next day's paper – a fair question in all conscience! At this time papers were reduced to very few pages and there was a shortage of old papers for fish and chips. Evidently one of our drivers had a friend in the trade and arranged to throw off a ten-quire bundle from his van when passing the shop.

By the end of the War, of the five directors who ran the business in 1939, two had died and one had retired. The hierarchy was then supposed to be Bartholomew, who became chairman in 1944, John Coope, who fairly quickly ceased to be significant, myself and James Cook, who had become our finance director. Bartholomew had qualifications which were valuable in the resuscitation of the editorial side of the *Mirror*, but he was no chairman. He might almost be called an anti-chairman. However, the editorial qualities of the two papers, aided by their politics, led to an increasing demand and to the *Mirror* springing into the lead as soon as their paper quota allowed, I think in 1947. During the War we urged a more vigorous pursuit of victory, and a due care for the interests of the other ranks in all three services. In fact we were what opposition the Government had in the war years. Attlee was merely supine, and the opposition consisted of Nye Bevan in the House of Commons and ourselves outside it. Our assessment of the political mood of the country was correct; that of the Government was not. The result was the Labour land-slide in 1945, to which Messrs Attlee, Bevin and Co. had contributed nothing. Though I did not expect a Labour victory at that time, it was obvious that the Conservative majority would be much reduced. Looking back, I think it would be fair to say that Labour would have won anyway. The arrogance and incompetence of Churchill's Government had seen to that, but the size of the Conservative débâcle owed much to the *Daily Mirror*, whose slogan was 'Vote for *him*', i.e. as your soldier husband, brother or father would wish you to vote.

From 1945 we supported the Government, though not uncritically. Bart's relations were with Herbert Morrison, my own more with Cripps. Both of them in their confidential moments groaned over the utter inadequacy of Attlee as PM, but while he had the support of Bevin he was immovable. I remember talking to someone who had been stuck between planes at some remote airport, and he and Attlee fell into conversation. They had nothing else to do for six hours, and Attlee held forth on Acton's dictum that all power corrupts and absolute power corrupts absolutely. He seemed obsessed by the problem. He was so afraid of being corrupted by power that in practice he just hoarded it, however he may have explained this to himself.

Though with no great enthusiasm, the *Mirror* supported the Labour Party in 1950 and was probably decisive in getting it a small majority, but it was not possible to keep such a poor thing alive for much longer, and it collapsed in 1951.

For the 1951 election Bart had adopted the slogan 'Whose finger on the trigger?', implying that peace was safer in Attlee's hands than in Churchill's. Churchill sued us for libel, but soon learned, as we knew, that our slogan was not libellous. However, he switched the charge to a piece we had printed earlier, given us in fact by the French Foreign Minister, that at a private dinner-party in Paris Churchill had advocated, under certain circumstances, a preventive war against the Russians. We had been given the story on the clear understanding that under no circumstances were we to reveal the source. As a result, when sued, we had no evidence and could only pay £1,500 to a charity nominated by Churchill. Our final brushes with Churchill were over saying that in the period 1951–5 Churchill was senile, and in no state to be Prime Minister. Lord Moran's book has

119

since revealed that our strictures were more than justified. The Tories kept him in office although he was far past his work, because they believed him to be a vote-winner for the Party.

In 1951 I became chairman of the *Mirror*. My primary worry was our Australian affairs, which I have dealt with elsewhere. The second consideration before us was to open a second printing plant in Manchester, so that we should be on level terms with the *Express* and the *Mail*, which had had one for many years. The *Mirror* had tried printing in Manchester in 1913 and had lost so much money that it had pulled out. My seniors had a very unhappy experience at that time and were determined not to repeat it. My chance came when the last of the old guard, Bartholomew, went and we were in a position to judge the move on its merits. In the thirties, when I first visited Manchester on business, the northern sale of the *Mirror* was about 60,000. We had at that time established a northern edition of the paper, but it was printed in London and could only have limited success. The northern print is now 1,300,000 or so, but there are still some twenty towns in the north where the *Express* is on top because we were so late in catering for their needs. For the northern readers sport is even more important than it is for men in the south. While Bart was chairman he not only took no interest in sport but he vetoed any attempt to give the subject reasonable coverage. However, with the northern print, we had to bring our sport into line with that of the *Express*, and better it if we could. This was a major move, as the extra expense was of the order of £7,000 a week, and extra revenue could only grow slowly from extra sale. It actually grew more slowly than it should have, as some of the features were much more suited to London readership than a Lancashire one. In fact it was not until we put Percy Roberts in charge of the northern operation many years later that we really began to push ahead.

Bart had had the idea of publishing a northern or a Scottish edition under a separate title, so that it should attract a separate advertising revenue. When I became chairman I thought I would resuscitate this idea in connection with the *Glasgow Record*, then owned by Kemsley Newspapers. We had one abortive round of negotiations, but eventually the deal went through. The Glasgow papers were doing badly, and we thought the *Record* and the *Sunday Mail* would serve as the Scottish editions of the *Mirror* and *Sunday Pictorial*. And so it has turned out. The *Mirror* sale in Scotland went down from about 100,000 to 25,000 and the *Record* sale went up from 340,000 to 530,000. On the other hand the *Sunday Pictorial* went down more than the *Sunday Mail* went up. This was presumably due to the competition of the *Sunday Post*, one of the phenomena of modern journalism. It is published by the firm of D. C. Thomson of Dundee, and looks like a newspaper that has strayed out of the 1920s. Some of the Scottish jokes are so Scottish they are unintelligible to Scots: some of the material so corny it is hardly true. But the paper on its own ground is immovably strong, and of recent years has been gaining ground in the north of England. In all the talk of newspapers and their proprietors, far too little credit has been given to Mr D. C. Thomson. Though he died at the age of ninety-one or so, I never met him, but always respect him as one of the great giants of our trade, and not only because of the success of the *Sunday Post*. His newspapers in Dundee and his children's comics may not have represented journalism as its most enlightened, but as a commercial publisher he had nothing to learn from anyone.

But to return to the *Glasgow Record*, which is in effect the Scottish edition of the *Daily Mirror*, with the advantage that it has its own advertisement revenue. As a result our Glasgow operation makes a handsome profit. In the package was the *Glasgow Evening News*, one of the three Glasgow evening papers at that time. In the long run there can only be one evening paper in Glasgow, and rather than incur losses for many years in the hope of being the sole survivor, we sold the *Evening News* to its rivals for £250,000, extinguishing in the process an annual loss of £180,000. What with this and that the purchase of the Glasgow business was a profitable and advantageous one. My colleagues thought my motives were nostalgic, as it was there that I started my career. I am not influenced by nostalgia but, in this case, by the prospect of a very advantageous extension of our business.

The profitability of this purchase was due to what has been called the priceless hidden asset of bad management, due to Lord Kemsley. When I arrived in Glasgow to take over, I was asked what to do about the garage roof. It appeared that it was made of glass, that the panes were loose and in a high wind were apt to drop out, and might fall and injure someone. I asked why this had not been attended to. It appeared that this required authority from London, and though letters had been sent over a period of six months, no answer had been received. I was also asked whether a weekly report on the *Sunday Mail* was required; one had been posted to London every Monday for seventeen years, but no acknowledgement or comment had been received. These were just examples of the over-centralization and mismanagement of the Glasgow business by Lord Kemsley. There are those who uphold his financial acumen, but to us at the *Mirror* he was always Groucho Kemsley (we thought he looked like one of the Marx Brothers), a figure of fun. He was very unlike his two elder brothers, Lord Camrose whom I knew slightly and Lord Buckland whom I did not know at all. Lord Buckland was said to be so much disliked by his staff that when he died out riding, a party was held to drink the health of the horse that killed him! But whether liked or disliked, he was immensely able.

Perhaps this is a good moment to interject the story of Hugh Cudlipp's departure from the *Mirror* in 1950 and his return in 1952. In the former year I had been in Lagos, and thought it would be an idea to look into the possibilities of sales for the *Daily Times* in Eastern Nigeria. I flew to Enugu and arrived in time for a strike in the coal mines there. I took a drive round the local centres of population, and was surprised by the crowds in the road through the mining villages. When I got back to the rest house one of the staff was standing on the steps with a carving-knife in his hand. I asked him why. He said, 'Your people have been killing mine'. The conversation then terminated, as I found a scorpion within a few inches of my foot. However, on enquiry it appeared there had been a riot and over a dozen miners had been killed. This was obviously a big story, and I prepared to go into the African town and hear what had really happened. However, I was assured that if I did so I would certainly not live to tell the tale, as the town was in a very angry mood. So I pieced together the story from anyone who had been present at the shooting and tried to cable it, but the cable office was shut. However, after heroic efforts by my companion Freddy Weston, we got the cable office open and prepared to send home my cable. This eventually reached the *Sunday Pictorial* office at 10 p.m. on Saturday night, the ideal hour for a newspaper scoop. I was rather pleased with my efforts, and returned to my hotel supposedly protected by watchmen with bows and arrows. When I got back to Lagos I found a cable from Bart asking why I had said nothing about the Enugu riots. It then came out that the cable had arrived in good time for publication and had not been used, though the story supplied the lead in the London papers on the following Monday, Tuesday and Wednesday. Hugh Cudlipp was on duty that night, and was not one in the ordinary way to miss a world scoop, but for reasons never explained spiked the story. I lost my one bid for a world scoop and Cudlipp was fired. He went to the *Sunday Express* where he spent two years kicking his heels before I, meanwhile having become chairman, invited him back, saying in my letter of invitation, 'Let's get together and make a dent in the history of our times.'

However, to return to the main stream of my story. We had now done or were doing all that was possible to develop our newspaper business, but meanwhile commercial television had come along. It seemed to me obvious that whatever might be the future of newspapers, television had a future of indefinite duration. But in the early stages television was bound to lose a lot of money. So it was surely prudent to stay out of the first round and come in when the original contractors had run out of money. The timing of this was critical, but luckily we bought our way into Associated Television at exactly the right moment. Moreover, the various interests represented on ATV covered electronics and popular show business, areas in which we lacked any knowledge. I think we can now say that the future of television seems more significant than appeared at that time, and we made a hatful of money as well. Some idea of this can be gleaned from the fact that when we acquired the Amalgamated Press, we had to sell their holding in Southern Television, and got forty-five pounds for shares that had cost one pound only three years earlier. This gives the measure of the huge capital profits made by the original contractors.

The next step in expanding the business was to get into magazines. It seemed that the Amalgamated Press (now Fleetway) controlled by Michael Berry and his family would sooner or later be in the market, and so it proved. He had enough on his hands with the *Daily Telegraph* without the Amalgamated Press, a very large enterprise in itself. The price we paid seemed a large one at the time, though Michael Berry told me his family had blamed him for letting the business go too cheap. Lord Camrose had acquired the shares from Northcliffe's executors in 1923. He had added the Kelly-Iliffe businesses to it, but in the thirty years it had been under Berry control much had been taken out of the business but not enough put back in. The first Lord Camrose was immensely able but selfish and greedy. By the time we acquired control the management of the various enterprises that constituted the Amalgamated Press was elderly, and the businesses themselves were running down. Financially the purchase proved a bonanza for us. The value of two subsidiaries, the Imperial Paper Mills and Kelly-Iliffe, was greater than the price we had paid for the whole. The consumer magazine part of the business, now called Fleetway, had thus cost us nothing and is currently making about £1,250,000 a year. Nevertheless we were left with serious problems, and those in the printing works are not entirely solved now.

One of the problems was that there were too many women's weeklies. The advertising available was spread too thin and the weaker ones would have to be weeded out. Odhams had recently taken over Newnes and was therefore by far the strongest operator in this field. After we had been in command for only a short time at Fleetway it became urgent to put through some degree of rationalization. So I approached Christopher Chancellor, at that time chairman of Odhams, to suggest that the women's magazines, or at any rate the women's weeklies, should all be put into a new company, in which Fleetway would have a minority interest. Christopher was understandably cool to this proposal and said, if he rejected the idea, would we make a bid for Odhams? I said, 'Perhaps'. Christopher thought this indicated a final intention and sought protection in the arms of Roy Thomson. A merger was worked out and announced on television. There on the screen were Roy and Christopher announcing their indissoluble marriage. The TV interrogator asked if there was any likelihood of a counter-bid. Roy said no one had the money to make one. This was a bit much, so I reached for the telephone, alerted my colleagues, and in fact we made a successful counter-bid. We should probably have done this anyway, but the stimulus that evening was Roy's remark. Naturally there were the usual cries of megalomania, but the deal was in itself a defensive one initiated through a misunderstanding. By buying Odhams, who had shortly before acquired Newnes and Hultons, we not only acquired the whole of the popular consumer magazines not already owned by Fleetway, but acquired the remaining two large publishers of trade and technical journals. These acquisitions certainly enabled us to rationalize the women's weeklies, but made us the biggest printers in the country. Some of our printing firms were efficient, others had fallen behindhand in modern technology, and some could only be closed. In any case too many were in London, where the restrictive practices of the unions were at their worst. It will have taken at least ten years from the Odhams deal before we shall be able to say that our printing works are up to an acceptable standard of efficiency.

The Odhams business had been very ably built up by Lord Southwood, who was efficient but was too mixed up in the affairs of Horatio Bottomley for his reputation to escape unscathed. When he died the management became fragmented and Parrack, in charge of the printing and labour relations, ran his side of the business as a separate enterprise. He had died just before we appeared on the scene, leaving a number of problems behind him. But all in all, Odhams was still a very strong business.

Newnes had been managed for years by Herbert Tingay, and he had retired shortly before our arrival, leaving the management in the hands of Hocking Baker. Their principal property was, and is, *Woman's Own*, a magazine built up by the editorial flair of James Drawbell, not the easiest man to work with, but one of the outstanding journalists of his time. Newnes, under the care principally of the people I have mentioned, was outstandingly well managed and mercifully had disposed of its printing works some years before.

The Hulton business was of course much smaller, and had suffered from the departure of the Reverend Marcus Morris, which took place before our time. Sir Edward Hulton, from his contribution to publishing, must have derived a fortune of not less than two million for himself and his family. Others whose contribution to the publishing industry might seem as great have enjoyed no such spectacular rewards.

With the acquisition of Odhams the expansion of the Mirror Group, now the International Publishing Corporation, was more or less complete. The group was now the largest firm of newspaper publishers, of consumer magazine publishers, of trade and technical magazine publishers and the largest employers of printing labour in the world. Big problems of rationalization, modernization and of efficient management confronted us, but further expansion in the periodical publishing world was no longer possible.

But there was one rapidly growing field of publishing in which we were neither strong nor efficient – book publishing, and in particular educational book publication. To make a beginning we acquired the firm of Ginn and Company and then looked round for someone to take charge of our books, an aspect of publishing of which we knew little. There are at present two major self-made publishers, Robert Maxwell and Paul Hamlyn. Robert Maxwell would not fit into a large organization except as its boss, but I arranged to meet Paul Hamlyn to see if he would join us and take our book publishing in hand, and this he is now doing. He was only thirty-seven when we paid two-and-a-quarter million for his business. He is a slight, shy figure and when you meet him it is hard to believe that he spent two years down a coal mine as a Bevin boy during the War, and that he is a wildly successful publisher of excellent books.

Since the early thirties I had sat on various committees of the Newspaper Proprietors' Association. This organization had been founded by Northcliffe as a breakaway body from the Master Printers' Federation. In his day Northcliffe was the accepted leader of Fleet Street, but on his death the NPA discussions were dominated by the mutual jealousies and hostilities between the *Daily Mail* and the *Daily Express*. Northcliffe himself had been keenly interested in labour matters, but the next generation of newspaper proprietors, Lords Beaverbrook, Rothermere and Camrose, were more interested in getting the paper out. In any case newspaper publishing was generally very profitable, so why have a show-down with the unions? Over a period of twenty-five years Esmond Rothermere was the chairman, with plenty of charm and some authority, but not, in my view, good at chairing a meeting. The vice-chairman in charge of labour matters was Fred Burnham. Though a pleasant social figure, he was a major disaster to the industry. I remember once saying of him that his idea of negotiation was to lie on the floor and invite the union general secretaries to come and kick him, which they very willingly did.

127

Naturally the weakness of the NPA cannot wholly be attributed to one man or one cause. The weakness of the Fleet Street newspapers was revealed at different times in all the different offices, including mine. The weakness of Fleet Street was essentially due to the fact that a daily newspaper has to come out every day and cannot make up for lost sales afterwards; it may well have lost some readers for good. But once the unions had wrung a concession from the London newspapers, little time was lost in pressing for the same concessions in the general trade, at least in London.

When Esmond Rothermere decided to retire from the chairmanship, there was naturally some speculation about his successor. I assumed I was out of the running, as Esmond is my cousin, and surely a change from the Harmsworth clan would be looked for. The *Daily Mirror* had been much too successful and had aroused a good deal of jealousy, and finally, some months earlier, I had said in public that the NPA showed all the courage and sense of purpose of a stranded jelly-fish! So imagine my astonishment when asked to lunch by Sir William Carr, chairman of the *News of the World*, and offered by those at the lunch the chairmanship of the NPA. I had been so critical in the past that I couldn't refuse, though of all my jobs in the publishing business this is the one I disliked most. The meetings deal with routine business, but every now and then there is a set piece with all the union representatives on one side of the table and the representatives of the management on the other. To conduct any aspect of negotiations under such circumstances is unsatisfactory, as one sometimes suspects that neither side might live up to its engagements. I said at the start I would take on the job for eighteen months, but finally got stuck with it for seven years.

When the first Royal Commission on the Press reported, it recommended a Press Council. The idea was very unwelcome to Fleet Street, but one was eventually set up under Lord Astor of Hever. This had no outside membership and to my mind served no purpose. So I refused to let our people take part.

When the second Royal Commission made the same recom-
mendation, only more emphatically, I felt something serious
had to be done. By that time I was chairman of the NPA and
if anything had to be done, I had to do it. Clearly there had to
be an independent chairman, preferably a retired judge. I didn't
know any retired judges except Lord Kilmuir. While contemplating this possibility I met Hartley Shawcross at a party
at the French Embassy and asked his advice. What did he think
of Lord Kilmuir for the job? He said he had a better suggestion.
I asked if he meant Hartley Shawcross. He laughed and said no.
The man he had in mind was Lord Devlin, who wanted to
retire from the Bench as soon as he had completed his fifteen
years and earned his full pension. But his name could not be
mentioned until nearer the date of his retirement, and until he
had cleared the matter with the Lord Chancellor. So I was at
first arguing on behalf of a 'legal luminary', name unknown even
to me, and later on behalf of a 'legal luminary' on whose
identity my lips were sealed. However, after a long struggle and
some considerable arm twisting all round I got the NPA, the
Newspaper Society and the Periodical Publishers' Association
as well as the lesser bodies to agree to the chairmanship of
Lord Devlin and the provision of the necessary funds. I think
Lord Devlin has done a wonderful job, not so much in correct-
ing the excesses of the Press, which are now inconsiderable, but
in restoring to a large extent the battered prestige of the newspapers. A similar body should be set up for television, or
perhaps one body with two committees for complaints, one for
the Press and the other for TV.

So much for a résumé of our commercial activities, which of
course occupy ninety-nine per cent of one's time. In the same
period, covering the first years of my chairmanship, politics
were at an uninteresting stage. From 1951 to 1955 Churchill
was Prime Minister. The elections of 1951, 1955 and 1959 had
been inevitable Tory victories, but there were moments of
interest.

After the purely negative qualities of Attlee, the arrival of a new leader of the Labour Party came as something of a tonic. Attlee had delayed his departure until there was no chance of Herbert Morrison succeeding him. Morrison, however, did not think he was too old to take over, and was bitterly hurt when he got a derisory vote for the leadership. I wrote him a friendly letter but got a reply saying that his defeat was due to me! This was, of course, nonsense. All we had done in the *Mirror* was to look forward in a general way to younger leadership.

Hugh Gaitskell and I had exactly the same background. Our fathers were in the Indian Civil Service: we were both at Winchester and Oxford. But even with all this in common, I found him a most difficult 'buttoned-up' character, except so it seems when he went dancing.

When we took up the Common Market, Hugh Gaitskell was fully in agreement, but at lunch some months later said that he had been talking to a Professor Meade and had decided the economic arguments were not sufficiently compelling, so he was going to oppose our joining the Common Market. I said I saw no reason to change my mind whatever Professor Meade might think. We parted on frosty, not to say hostile terms, Hugh apparently thinking that if he changed his mind so should I.

The Labour Party front bench at that time was not conspicuous for its range of ability, and furthermore in 1954 both Alfred Robens and George Brown were planning to leave politics and return to work with their respective unions. So I arranged for them each to be paid £500 a year, later increased, as consultants to make it possible for them to stay in politics. I later did the same thing for the same reason for Richard Marsh, but nobody else. Robens never made any secret of this but George Brown's arrangement was not publicly known until it finally leaked out years later, causing him some embarrassment.

The big event in the middle fifties was Suez. I think about two months before the landing I had had an hour with Harold Macmillan, then the Chancellor of the Exchequer. He left me in no doubt that a military operation was being planned. This seemed to me insane, and I said so. Macmillan's argument was that the moment our troops landed, Nasser would fall and be replaced by a leader more friendly to ourselves. I said this was not how things worked. The first British soldier to land would inevitably consolidate support for Nasser. Macmillan said I obviously had no idea how many enemies he had. I said that whether they were friends or enemies, in the face of a threat from the foreigner they would rally round their leader. In any case if we chased him out of Egypt, he would set up a Government in exile in some other Arab country and direct guerilla warfare all over Egypt. To cope with such a situation we should need half a million men, and where were they coming from? I did not succeed in shaking Mr Macmillan's opinion. It was astonishing to me that a professional politician should show so little understanding of politics. Mr Wilson has made exactly the same mistake over Rhodesia, apparently unaware that the more he attacks Mr Ian Smith the more he strengthens Smith's position.

Following on this conversation and on confirmation from other contacts, we really got to work to head off this act of lunacy. Hugh Gaitskell was convinced the Government was bluffing and that it was his duty to help them bluff. It took a lot of persuading to convince him that the Government was not bluffing. Hence a rather sudden change of attitude by the Labour Party at one point. Hugh Cudlipp went down to Brighton to the TUC Conference and persuaded them to pass a resolution hostile to any military intervention, and meanwhile our paper got up to every antic we could think of to persuade the Government to call off this adventure.

It was interesting that over this whole enterprise the *Guardian*, the *Observer* and the *Mirror* pursued much the same policy. The *Mirror* lost net about eighty thousand sale, the *Observer*, which had been gaining on the *Sunday Times*, fell away and has been far behind ever since. But the *Guardian* actually gained sale. The attitude of many of our readers was that they were against military ventures, but that once our troops were involved they must be supported.

The next big event was the election of 1964. At one point it had seemed possible that Labour could win in 1959, but an ill-timed bus strike altered the political trend and by the time the election was in sight, it was clear the Tories were home and dry. By 1964 the Tories had been in office for thirteen years, which is really too long if the British Parliamentary system is to work. It is difficult to recruit good MPs if there is no prospect of office, and the longer a party is out of office the more ignorant and irresponsible its criticisms are likely to be. By 1964 Labour had a new chief in Harold Wilson, who was a brilliant Leader of the Opposition and who, at that stage, was readier to listen. The Tories had run their term of office right to the statutory five years, which is generally a mistake. I was not particularly impressed by the promise of a Labour Government, but quite convinced that it was time for a change. It seemed to me that if we supported Sir Alec Douglas-Home, a difficult manoeuvre but possible, he would win. If we went flat out for Labour, they might win. It would be a close run thing, and the attitude of the *Mirror* would be decisive. So we decided to go all out for Labour and see if it could be done and it was, just.

Apart from the commercial and political effects at the *Mirror* we realized that such a large and rich organization had a responsibility to culture and the arts. Our first effort was under Bart's régime when we bought *Public Opinion* of which Connor was made the editor. The idea was that we should channel into it a lot of the more highbrow material available at the *Mirror* office but not suitable for the *Mirror*. Connor was a great journalist but not a great editor. Nevertheless, I don't think the venture deserved to fail as dismally as it did. Another venture of about the same time was the National Exhibition of Children's Art. This started as a very modest editorial promotion (prize three guineas!), but was so successful that we got Sir Herbert Read to get an appropriate committee together and made it a permanent institution with a definite educational purpose. This has been a huge success: the exhibits have travelled the world, it has been imitated in foreign countries, and has really helped in raising the standard of art teaching in this country. I remember one teacher wrote in and said that at her school art teaching was held in such low regard that she was not allowed in the common-room during the morning break. She had had to hide in the lavatory. But now one of her pupils had won one of our awards her prestige had soared, and she was now a full member of the common-room.

Towards the end of his time Bart saw at a cinema a performance of a Californian Youth Orchestra. He thought this a suitable promotion for the *Mirror* with its dependence on young people. However, he could not find out how to organize such a thing and his interest lapsed. When I became chairman I revived the idea and asked Philip Zec, who had friends in the musical world, to find out how it could be done. He returned to say there already was such an orchestra, the National Youth Orchestra, which was very highly regarded but very short of funds. This is how we came to be connected with the National Youth Orchestra, by a long chalk the best thing of its kind in the world.

Somewhere around the same date my old friend Rosamund Lehmann pointed out that there was then no purely literary publication, and in fact a young poet found it very difficult to get his poems printed at all. This seemed a useful piece of do-gooding, and the *London Magazine* was floated with John Lehmann, Rosamund's brother, as editor. He had had a great success during the War with *New Writing* but failed to repeat its success with the *London Magazine*. When it was clear it was making little progress the publication was made over to John Lehmann as a gift. It still continues under other ownership.

Having failed with the *London Magazine* we made a different sort of literary effort next time, the children's literary competition. This has been a success, though not of the same order as its musical and artistic counterparts. The real idea behind these promotions is two-fold; from the cultural point of view to improve the standard of teaching in the schools and from the commercial point of view to make a favourable impression among important people whose favourite newspaper reading was not the *Daily Mirror*. Finding child geniuses is not the objective.

Our last and by a long way our most expensive cultural effort was the *Statist*. The idea here was the same as it had been with *Public Opinion*. Surely it would be possible to use the political and diplomatic information that flows into the *Mirror* office, but cannot be used by the *Daily Mirror*, in a publication which would give the *Economist* something to worry about. In Paul Bareau we thought we had the ideal editor. For whatever reason we lost a lot of money and never got the sale above twelve thousand. It ended nearer eight thousand.

However, what about something scientific or quasi-scientific? When I came to examine the possibilities in this sphere I found that any promising lines of research were being undertaken already, and anyway needed huge sums of money to get anywhere. But I had for many years been interested in telepathy, not that I have any telepathic gifts myself, though I know some who have. Apart from the fact that this is a neglected area of enquiry, my own special interest in the subject is broadly that our present materialist civilization is getting us to a dead end, of which the hydrogen bomb is the most obvious symbol. If civilization is to put the material back into its proper proportion, this must be done by offering something else. You cannot beat something with nothing, as the Americans say. Telepathy is an experience most people have had. If, beginning with telepathy, you could arouse wide interest in ESP you would be getting away from what can be weighed and measured to the intangible, which includes such experiences as happiness and beauty, which themselves are not reproducible at will.

I got the firm to finance a small group of research workers in this field in Oxford under the leadership of Miss Celia Green, and also gave some financial support to Professor Beloff at Edinburgh University and to the Society for Psychical Research. The sums involved were quite modest, and even if no significant discoveries are made, these centres of interest in the subject now exist – in London as before, but in Oxford and Edinburgh as well.

Part Two

Part Two

Government Service

In 1948 I was summoned by Herbert Morrison, then Lord President of the Council and invited to be chairman of the British Film Institute, an organization I had not previously heard of. I have always felt the country has a first claim on one's time, and if this is what the Government of the day wanted me to do, I would have a go. The Institute had sixteen governors, was managed by the secretary, Oliver Bell, and was concerned with the keeping of the National Film Archives and fostering film societies and generally encouraging the study of films as an art form. I took over the chairmanship from Patrick Gordon Walker who expressed doubts to me about the suitability of Mr Bell for his job. I had not been long in the chair before it became plain that Mr Bell was not the right man, and that whatever other virtues Mr Gordon Walker might have administration was not his strong suit. The sixteen governors were nominated to represent various interests in the cinematograph industry, and others supposed to have the artistic qualities of the cinema at heart. There was no common interest binding these people together as there is in a board of directors and, of course, I had had no hand in their selection. So chairing the meetings was a considerable test. I have always held that chairmanship is a special skill, and not a very common one at that. In this case the solution seemed to me to be to keep the meetings short, I mean not more than an hour and a half, and the test of interest was the average attendance, which I think worked out at about twelve out of sixteen.

Anyway, one of the first jobs was to find a successor to Oliver Bell in a field with which I was quite unfamiliar. So I invited John Grierson to lunch and asked him if he knew of anyone suitable. Grierson had invented the documentary film and was a major figure in the Film Institute world. He said much the best man would be Denis Forman, now managing director of Granada. We had, of course, advertised this job but Denis had not applied for it. Grierson said he would try and persuade Denis to apply, which he eventually did on the last day before applications closed. When we came to examine the short list, it boiled down to two applicants, Denis Forman and Wolf Mankowitz. I favoured Mankowitz, then entirely unknown, but the majority were right in choosing Denis Forman. Mankowitz has always been very appreciative that I believed in him when he had made no name for himself. Denis Forman was a huge success, and after his appointment all I had to do was to support him while he transformed the Institute. His great achievement was the founding of the National Film Theatre, which has had a number of vicissitudes but seems now to be very firmly established.

In 1951 the Labour Government lost the election, and from then on I had to deal with Lord Woolton, the Tory President of the Council. He was a wonderful flatterer. During a conversation with him you felt you were being wrapped round with folds and folds of warm silk. I tried to persuade him that the Film Institute, a body largely existing on public funds, was really too small to be independent. Surely it should either be merged in the Central Office of Information with other Government film activities, or with the Arts Council with other artistic patronage. It is typical of ministerial reaction to suggestions that my point was ignored. Suggestions to Ministers are seldom rejected, they are just ignored. Though this is boorish ill manners, it perhaps has the advantage of leaving no actual rejection on the file.

The British film industry was my first introduction to the crazy world of Treasury finance. Once a year we had to draw up a forecast of our expenditure for eighteen months ahead. As it was quite impossible to foresee our expenditure so far into the future, you put in for the maximum that you could hope would be taken seriously. It also had to be set out under a number of heads, ten to twelve I seem to remember. As transfer from one head to another was not allowed, you put in for the maximum under each head. These extravagant claims were, of course, cut down without consultation, so that some of the sums we were allowed were surprisingly high. However, in due course you found you were nearing the end of the financial year with useful sums unspent under some heads. Hence February and March were devoted to spending, as any shortfall in expenditure would lead to a cut-back next year, when conditions might be very different. The whole process made extravagance obligatory, and though I understand the system has been modified, one still hears of hospitals desperately buying unwanted equipment in March so as to get rid of their allocation of money for the financial year. The obvious plan would be to encourage these institutions to save by allowing them to spend say half of any savings on some pet project that had not been approved.

Though I think the four years I was chairman of the Film Institute were successful ones, I was never invited by the Government to chair any other similar body. Was this forgetfulness on the part of the civil servants? Or had I trodden on some important ministerial or official toe? I don't know.

Twelve years rolled by, and the election of 1964 was coming up. I was asked independently by George Brown and by Jim Callaghan if I would be prepared, if they won the election, to serve the new Government in any way. I said, as before, that I thought the country had first claim on my time and that I would help in any way in which I felt qualified to help. George never asked my advice or invited me to help in any way, but Jim asked if I would like to be a director of the Bank of England. I said, yes. There was then a long delay until Jim rang me up in New York and told me the Bank was resisting my appointment strongly but he was being firm. Apparently Rowley Cromer fought me off for two months but eventually gave way, so that I was appointed a week after my term of office started. I never gathered why Rowley objected. We had been on friendly terms, he had married my cousin, and I was a chairman of two big companies. I should have expected him to sigh with relief that he had not been asked to accommodate Kaldor or Balogh.

I enjoyed my three years as a director of the Bank. The directors have been surrounded with an entirely bogus aura of knowledge and power. The Bank is run by the Governor, the Deputy-Governor and the Chancellor of the Exchequer. There are four other executive directors, some of whom are and some of whom are not important. The twelve non-executive directors I suppose can theoretically control the Bank, but then the Government of the day can issue a binding instruction. In practice neither happens. The Governor and the Chancellor decide what is to be done and the Court concurs. It is not consulted and seldom informed. For two months I was on the Committee of Treasury which is a sort of inner circle of the Court. But as a Committee we were told very little and consulted not at all. I am not objecting to this, as any attempt by outside directors to run the Bank could only be either futile or disastrous. Bank Rate is by statute within the authority of the Court, though in fact they are only told what has already been agreed between the Governor and the Chancellor. Exchange control is regarded as the business of a customer (the Government!!) and so directors are not entitled to know about transactions on Government account. Personally, I think directors of nationalized bodies may on occasion be able to offer useful advice, but in general they can only be there to see the business is properly run and, if it is not, to report to the Minister responsible so that something can be done. As a member of the Court I sat on the staff committee, and thereby met the more important members of the staff, and on the Debden Committee which is responsible for the printing of our Treasury notes. In this way one could judge the Bank as an organization, and I came to it with a very fresh eye, as newspaper publishing is as far removed from central banking as it is possible to get. The Bank is still the creation of Montague Norman. Whatever mistakes he made over monetary policy, he did a wonderful internal job at the Bank. The staff are happy and competent. Good young men receive early promotion, and women can look for promotion at any rate to very near the top and to very nearly the same pay as men. The administration is a bit lavish and very jealous of its independence. I believe the Treasury does not know, at least officially, the pay of the executive directors, which by the standard of other nationalized industries is high. The information and judgement provided by the economic intelligence department struck me as extraordinarily good. During my three years the Bank's forecasts were consistently right (though gloomy): Ministers were invariably optimistic and wrong. As a result the Bank had the frustrating experience of proffering good advice that was pretty consistently rejected.

When the Labour Government came into office the question of devaluation was mooted and Wilson quite rightly rejected the idea. His reason, he told me, was that sterling had twice been devalued under Labour Governments and a third devaluation would be very damaging to Labour's image. I don't accept this as a valid reason. The attitude of the Bank was consistently against devaluation. Their argument had nothing to do with 'sacred cows' or the gnomes of Zurich. It was that if the Government finds it hard to contain inflation before devaluation, how can they hope to do so afterwards? I find this argument conclusive. In any case, in 1964 our price level was not out of line with other countries. It was overseas expenditure on Government account that was wrecking our balance of payments.

One would suppose the Bank of England would be a rather stuffy institution with promotion by seniority and a preference for quill pens over typewriters. But this was far from the case. I have already mentioned the rapid promotion given to young men of promise, but the Bank pioneered in the use of computers, particularly for the stock registers. At the printing works, they were developing with the manufacturers printing machines that would print and number pound notes from paper in reels. Though I am not an admirer of the artistic qualities of our notes, they are very hard to forge, much harder than American currency notes.

My introduction to the Bank was necessarily pretty cool, but when their fears, whatever they may have been, were seen to be unfounded, Rowley Cromer, then the Governor, and the other directors could not have been more friendly. Any value in being a Bank director lies in the personal contacts you make, mostly at lunch and not only with the directors and with senior members of the staff, but also with the chairmen of the clearing banks and the acceptance houses and so on.

I suppose if you wanted to criticize, it would be that the Bank is too prepared to accept the existing set-up of the City and too reluctant to take the initiative in modernizing it. It was slow to realize that much of the traditional function of the banks was being taken over by the Building Societies, hire purchase finance houses and other institutions. It has also seemed to me that the City provides a lavish living for too many charming men of no discernible ability. It could be argued in fact that the City is the last stronghold of the old school tie. Though a wearer of one of the best of the old school ties myself, I have always been very critical of the public school network and have been regarded, I dare say rightly, as a renegade from their ranks because I think promotion should be by merit and not by reasons of friendships formed in boyhood.

My next appointment was to the National Parks Commission by Mr Willey, one of the Ministers I had never met. I don't know why I was chosen. I did for thirty years own a property of five thousand acres in Aberdeenshire, and for a shorter period one thousand acres in Cumberland, and I am a country lover, but I had never taken any active part in the preservation of the countryside, however desirable I know it to be. I have been too busy to make any contribution to the Commission, at any rate so far.

The Coal Board, like the Bank of England, is another

nationalized body, but there the resemblance stops. Whereas at the Bank we were provided with almost no information that was not public knowledge, at the Coal Board we are deluged with information; one would think they have an affiliated paper mill, so copious is the flow of paper providing information on every conceivable aspect of the coal-mining industry. At first I was intrigued to get documents labelled 'Secret'. These came in envelopes marked 'Secret' and inside was another envelope marked 'Secret'. But I soon learned that the contents in any other enterprise would be labelled 'Confidential' and some of the 'Secret' communications are hardly even that.

The Coal Board never meets as such. It consists of about eight men who bear the responsibility. But at the monthly Coal Board meetings we are joined by twenty or thirty of the top executives and are then addressed by Lord Robens as if we were a public meeting. We are not consulted but we are very fully informed.

Richard Marsh, the Minister of Fuel and Power, who appointed me, told a friend of mine that he had appointed me as a counterweight to Lord Robens, and was deeply disappointed to find that I was his ally. He apparently thought the other members of the Coal Board were so dominated by Robens that it was important to have in me someone who was not. This is of course to misunderstand the possible rôle of a part-time director of a nationalized industry. He can only watch what goes on and report to the Minister if the industry is being mismanaged. Actually I think the country is fortunate to have Lord Robens as chairman of the Coal Board. It is the combination of Robens and Paynter, the admirable secretary of the National Union of Mineworkers, that has enabled the contraction of the coal-mining industry to take place as smoothly as it has. I would not run the meetings of the Coal Board as Lord Robens does, but that is irrelevant. Every chairman must run the business for which he is responsible in the way suited to his temperament, and he is entitled to be judged by the results. By this standard Lord Robens emerges with all colours flying.

When I was appointed to the Bank of England by Jim Callaghan I supposed he would on occasion seek my opinion on this or that aspect of the Bank's affairs. But this was not so, and on the occasion when I offered my opinions they were ignored. Marsh did once ask me to see him about the Coal Board, but the conversation was swiftly diverted into other channels, mostly his difficulties with the steel industry. Without seeking tales out of school, I should have thought an occasional chat with the part-time directors you have yourself appointed would not be out of place.

West Africa

I have been trying to recall the story of our West African ventures. At some time during 1946 someone came to see Bart and suggested that we should start a newspaper in Nigeria. I was never told who he was, and he disappeared from the story immediately he had made the suggestion. Bart hinted that the idea was semi-official, which it may well have been. We were frustrated at that time as no development was possible in the British newspaper field owing to newsprint rationing. So the proposal was attractive in principle. A senior executive was sent out to investigate, travelled around a good deal, came back impressed with the possibilities, and suggested we should start our paper in Ibadan. However, further enquiries showed that one of the Lagos dailies, the *Daily Times*, had been founded in 1926 and was owned in Liverpool. I pressed for the purchase of the paper and its two off-shoots, *West Africa* and *West African Review*, arguing that it is easier to resuscitate an existing newspaper than to start a new one. This was agreed, and we paid £46,000 for the little group, which was making about £2,000 a year. Clearly, any revival would involve capital expenditure and a loss on trading for some years. The newspaper was selling about 6,000: *West Africa* about 850 : the *Review* made most of such profits as there were. We actually acquired the business in December 1947. Shortly afterwards I went out for the first time, and was in Accra just before the riots of February 1948. On my return I was put in charge of the West African venture and have remained intimately concerned until

147

quite recently. I was given this responsibility to keep me busy
and away from the office, but for me it was a fascinating
experience to be a close and privileged observer of emergent
Africa.

The newspaper I took over was badly printed on a flat-bed
press in a small office in Broad Street, Lagos. The London
manager I had inherited from the old owners was Freddy
Weston. Some changes had been made by our people before I
took over. The main problems, however, of management and of
politics, had not been gone into. The principal papers then
were the *Pilot*, the organ of Zik and the National Council for
Nigeria and the Cameroons, and the *Daily Service*, the organ of
those Yorubas who did not support the National Council.
Clearly, a foreign-owned paper could not be partisan; its readership would have to be African and its policy would have to be
in favour of self-government. The other papers were filled with
partisan politics, mainly personal abuse of the other side.
Obviously therefore we should have to print more news. The
staff were always inclined to print too much foreign news, which
you could pick up on the radio, rather than scour the country
for local stories, a very much more difficult undertaking in
Nigeria. The papers published no sport, no women's page, no
readers' letters. But putting first things first, the most important
thing was sport. In a country obsessed with highly emotional
politics, the most effective way of lowering the temperature
seemed to me to fill the national stage with as many non-
politicians as possible. Hence sport and, at suitable seasons,
religion, both Christian and Moslem. Sex was not important,
as the African public were firm believers in 'do it yourself'.
Later, with the growth of feminine fashions, this has become
less true. Crime was of little interest except when one of the
secret societies was involved, when you had a very big story
indeed on your hands. In any case, with a very inflammable,
emotional public it was not desirable to give any great prominence to crime. As we soon became by far the most popular
paper, I could set my own standards of what we should print.

I suppose the main reason for our early success was our excellent network of distribution. The African papers did, and still do, produce their newspapers when they feel so disposed, and then send them out regardless of the hour of arrival within reach of the customer. I found that in Nigeria people started moving about at first light, about six in the tropics, so the newspaper had to be produced to arrive at the principal centres of population at six. There was no means of conveyance, so we developed a bus service which carried passengers and freight as well as our newspapers. When we could keep thieving of fares within reasonable limits, the bus service paid its way and the papers were carried for nothing. This bus service became quite an institution and, before the recent troubles, was covering 2,600 miles a day. To make the buses conspicuous I had them painted yellow with *Daily Times* in red. Naturally our buses had to run to a definite time-table and we had to have reliable drivers. So the bus service acquired a reputation, and at one time there were two rival bus services, both painted red and yellow and with the names of fictitious newspapers (one of them *Daily Mirror*) to give their services more plausibility!

When I arrived in Lagos I immediately came up against the recurrent difficulty of running a newspaper in West Africa. Before I took over, a *Daily Mirror* sub-editor had been appointed editorial director (the editor, even in those days, was always an African). At home this man was a stolid reliable Scot, one would have thought just the man for the job. But within a few weeks he had got mixed up with African women, was drinking heavily and had even managed to get entangled with some *ju-ju* men. His work, of course, suffered and he was sent home, to be taken back as stone sub on the *Daily Mirror*, where he gave no trouble until his death fifteen years later. Why over forty per cent of the men we sent to West Africa went to pieces, sometimes within days, was never clear to me. I suppose they suddenly found they were more important than they ever could be at home and just couldn't take it. On the

149

other hand, those who did win through were shown to be pure gold, and now have a large share in the top management of the IPC Group. Though men were hired for a specific function, the European staff was so small that when they got out there the journalist might be called on to get the rotary press going – in fact everyone had on occasion to turn his hand to anything.

Apart from all the usual problems in running a newspaper anywhere, we had the additional problem of witchcraft. I had lunch with Alfred Osula one day, he was then a director and manager, and I noticed he had two black dogs. I made some comment and he said that when they had difficulty with the rotary press they would sacrifice to Ogun, God of Iron, and away the press would go. I asked what the ceremony consisted of and he said you made a pile of old iron in the machine room, poured on it a libation of gin, and then sacrificed a black dog, pouring its blood over the pile. This ceremony was quite harmless, and I never knew whether Alfred believed in it as fervently as his staff.

Ther were *ju-ju* men who were prepared to bring illness for a fee. There were rainmakers, who could also keep rain off, or so it was said – most valuable in the wet season! I was never in Africa long enough to have any experience myself, but those who had lived in the bush all had strange stories to tell, of news travelling faster than by telegram, of enemies brought to a slow death, and so on. Talking to Milton Margai at a football match when he was Prime Minister of Sierra Leone I heard they had difficulty in preventing small boys climbing the trees round the Freetown football ground and seeing the game for nothing. So a magician was brought in, and at the next match several boys fell out of the trees and were hurt, so the evil of non-paying fans was abated! The PM said he was scouring the country for magicians for the impending visit of the Queen, but he was having little success, as young men these days did not go in for magic! I took my wife Ruth to see a fetish priestess on the escarpment east of Dodowa. She was a nice woman with a spiritual quality of some sort, but it was difficult to say what sort. Asked how a priestess was chosen, she said that when the old priestess died the new one declared herself within a period of months. She might be an adult or a child, but it would be clear to the workers at the shrine that this was the successor. This sounded very like the method of selection of the Dalai Lama.

When on my first visit to Lagos, I stayed with Hugh Foot, now Lord Caradon. He had just arrived to take up his post as Chief Secretary and we lived in his official house, now pulled down, while he awaited the arrival of his furniture. We were together for ten days before I moved on, and his furniture arrived in the good ship *Sobo*. He remained Chief Secretary for two and a half years or so before moving on to Jamaica as Governor. The Governor of Nigeria was Sir John McPherson, who had been given Nigeria, one of the top three Governorships, as his first Governorship. He twice had his term of office extended. Foot's position in Nigeria was one of great importance at that time, and to move from the centre of African affairs right out to the periphery seemed to me to show an astonishing lack of judgement. But then it has seemed to me at intervals since that while I like Mac (as Hugh was called), and he is clearly very intelligent, he sometimes lacks judgement.

One day we were looking at the *Daily Times* at breakfast, and at that time it was a poor paper, badly printed. Hugh Foot told me there is an Arab proverb, 'To its mother even a beetle is beautiful'! On my first visit I was asked out to dinner by different officials every night: on subsequent visits I was largely ignored except by the Governor of the day who always asked me to lunch or to dine. The reason for the attitude of the white officials was that the paper aimed to have an African readership and advocated self-government. Though this last had been official policy for forty years, no attempt to implement it locally was made. Governors were usually judged by their despatches home, and not by their performance on the spot. Another Governor I remember was Armitage, when he was Finance

151

Minister of the Gold Coast. I was assured he would soon be a Governor. When he was appointed a Governor, it was to Cyprus he was sent, with instructions to have no dealings with Makarios. He stayed there only a few weeks and was moved on to Nyasaland, where the unpolitical Armitage was left to cope with a purely political problem.

As Governors were judged apparently by their despatches home, so Colonial Secretaries were judged by their performance in the House of Commons. Someone once said to me what a good Colonial Secretary Lennox-Boyd was. I said he seemed good at his public relations, but otherwise ineffective. Viewed from West Africa he had no discernible policy, and I thought his choice of officials to carry out any policy he might have had was erratic. Ah, was the reply, but you should see him at the Despatch Box!

Colonial Secretaries came and went, but the man who was more important than any or all of them was one Ralph Furse, responsible for recruiting for the Colonial Service from 1930 to 1948, after which date he was retained as an adviser. His idea of the suitable recruit was a man with a public school background, a degree at Oxford or Cambridge, preferably with second-class honours, and, if possible, a blue or some other sign of athletic prowess. In 1910 in West Africa this type was not unsuitable. They had to take over when very young a huge area of undeveloped Africa and cope. They were often far from anyone whose advice they could seek: in the early days there was a grave risk to their health: if they married, their children had to be brought up at home. You needed brave, self-reliant men. But as time went on and the country was opened up, more and more Africans were educated in England and returned to the Coast as barristers or as graduates of the London School of Economics. The old type of colonial civil servant could not cope with these new-style Africans and, in any case, had a training and a tradition that made him allergic to politics and, of course, in the higher walks of colonial administration from 1945 onwards, the job was substantially a political one. Hugh Foot could

1960. Christmas in Lagos, Nigeria. Cecil King presenting a gift to
the son of one of his employees at a staff party in the premises of the
Nigerian Daily Times, of which he was Chairman.

1967. Cecil King in Lagos being greeted by General Gowon, Supreme Commander of the Nigerian Forces.

cope with the new situation because of his family background.

In the early days in Nigeria the only generally well-known politician was Zik, who usually wouldn't see me. In fact, until he became Governor-General, I had only met him about twice. On one occasion he gave me lunch at Government House and was hilariously funny in describing his experiences canvassing in Yoruba country. Zik was a born journalist and could make good speeches in Ibo (he was an Ibo), in Hausa (he was brought up in the North), in Yoruba (he had lived in the West for most of his life), in English, and I believe in French. Awolowo was at that time a barrister on the fringes of politics. I tried to get him to write a fortnightly column for the paper, but he thought it would be politically unwise, and he probably did not need the money. Akintola, subsequently murdered when Premier of the West, was a journalist. He applied to me for the job of editor of the *Daily Times* at thirty-five pounds per month. I didn't think he was good enough and did not give him the job. However, he bore me no ill-will, and when he was Premier was very hospitable whenever I was in Ibadan.

Britain's cardinal error when giving Nigeria self-government was to have a federation of three regions in which the North, the most backward in many ways, could outvote the other two. The outstanding civil servant in the North in my day was Rex Niven who never got the promotion to which his great ability entitled him. He told me he had put forward a scheme for splitting the North into three in 1937, but it was turned down as 'premature', which it clearly was not.

The Lieutenant-Governor of the East in my early days was Bernard Carr, with whom I stayed in Enugu. He was very able, and when about to retire was very anxious that the Secretary of the East, Brigadier Gibbons, should succeed him. However, McPherson thought otherwise and appointed one Pyke-Nott. Gibbons, believed to be the ablest colonial servant then serving in Nigeria, was sent as Commissioner to the Cameroons, where his great ability was almost totally wasted.

Britain's occupation of Nigeria in the early days had been a progressive influence bringing peace, better communications and some education, but certainly by the thirties had been a purely negative one. To start with, there was no real policy except that of keeping on keeping on. When I was first in Nigeria, the tour of duty was fifteen months on the Coast followed by three months' leave. To avoid the difficulties of leave reliefs, the absurd system had grown up by which out in the bush a man never returned to the same area. An African's loyalty is to a person, not to a government, and this meant that the Africans had to get used to a new boss every fifteen months. Moreover, every District Officer knew that if he could postpone a decision for a maximum of fifteen months, the problem would fall into someone else's lap. A new man started in the bush and was then given a turn in the secretariat. If he was good he remained in the secretariat, getting more and more out of touch with the Africans, whose welfare was the object of the whole exercise. When I said I thought the Navy had such a good idea in that an officer to gain promotion had to do a turn at sea in every rank, Foot couldn't see the point. Needless to say, the men in the bush felt this very strongly, as they had to wrestle with secretariat characters whose sojourn in the bush was long ago, and who were more familiar with paper than with people. And of course there were the individual acts of lunacy: like the man who learnt Sobo (now called Urhobo) and claimed to be one of only five Englishmen who had ever learnt the language; but after getting his interpretership, he was never afterwards posted to an area where Sobo was spoken.

For much of the time in which I was active in Nigeria, the three leaders of the country were Zik of the Ibos and the East, Awolowo of the Yorubas and the West, and the Sardauna of Sokoto in the North. Zik was a politician to his finger-tips but no administrator. I thought Awolowo had little political sense, but was an energetic administrator, and was not personally corrupt. The North was dominated by the Sardauna of Sokoto, a most impressive aristocrat, fully six foot seven in height, nephew and presumed successor of the Sultan of Sokoto, the leader of all Nigerian Moslems. The late Sardauna was no administrator, lazy and corrupt. The natural alliance in political terms would have been the North and the West, the more conservative of the three main tribes. But in a rash moment Awolowo had made public a claim to Ilorin, and in an even less prudent moment had cast doubt on the then Sardauna's ancestry. The second was an insult which could never be forgiven, and the first was a claim which could not have been realized at that time or until quite recently. In the Ilorin emirate there are some hundreds of thousands of Yorubas, and the idea of redrawing the boundary between North and West so as to restore these people to their fellow tribesmen was sensible in itself, but should be advanced cautiously and at the right time. Awolowo's lack of political sense was not helped by McPherson's personal hostility.

When the *Daily Times* had been established as by far the most important paper in Nigeria, I thought we should be useful to the Government at home in carrying the country forward to self-government. But this proved not to be the case over any of the West African colonies, or later over the Caribbean. Successive Secretaries of State preferred official information, and were completely uninterested in anything from any other source. I found this hard to understand. Why not accept help? It would cost nothing. Surely it was important to check official information by news and views from some other source.

It was my custom when in Nigeria to ask different members of the staff to lunch to get to know them better. One of the abler journalists some years ago was Babatunde Jose, and when I invited him to lunch with me he declined on the grounds that it was Ramadan and he was fasting during the daytime. I thought this was very strong-minded of him and admired him for it. So I sent for him and asked him if he would like to go on a pilgrimage to Mecca, the duty of every devout Moslem. It appeared that there was nothing more important in his eyes, so off he went to the three great objects of Mohammedan veneration, Mecca, Medina and Jerusalem. He was also to look in on the great Moslem university in Cairo. Jose is the great-grandson of a Yoruba slave in Brazil, who managed to get back to Nigeria. There were a number of slaves who achieved this, so much so that there is a Brazilian quarter of Lagos and there are a number of old houses built in a Brazilian style.

Jose returned to Lagos a *hajji*, or pilgrim, and as such wears a distinctive head-dress at Friday prayers and enjoys enhanced prestige throughout the African community. However, he took his experience very seriously, gave up his small consumption of beer and cigarettes and emerged as one of the more stable national figures in the trials and tribulations through which Nigeria has gone of late. He is now chairman and managing director of the Nigerian venture, which consists not only of newspapers and magazines but also a flourishing general printing division and a profitable packaging enterprise, the whole making profits well in excess of £100,000 per annum.

In 1949 we acquired a business started by the clients of a London firm of stockbrokers. It was intended to publish a paper in Accra, but the enterprise was failing and we took it over at a discount. Eventually, in 1950, the *Daily Graphic* was launched, the only daily paper I have founded. Before it appeared, the chiefs were going to declare a boycott, so I attended a meeting of the paramount chiefs at Dodowa and made a speech which decided them not to impose a boycott. However, out of the frying-pan into the fire! The Nationalist Party, known as the Convention People's Party, declared a boycott, so that our initial sale, instead of 10,000, was only 2,000. However, before long the Accra races came along, and aided by the tips of the local manager of National Cash Register, we gave five out of seven winners. From that day the boycott was forgotten and the *Graphic* forged ahead, eventually to a larger sale than its Nigerian partner. Owing to gold mines and cocoa, the Gold Coast had been richer than Nigeria and therefore better educated. At least that was the explanation that occurred to me. Anyway, it was true that it was far easier to recruit and train a competent African staff in Accra than in Lagos. Part of this might be due to the fact that the Ewes, the tribe that occupies the territory to the east of Accra, appeared to be the most intelligent and most adaptable of all the tribes we had to deal with. So much was this so, that we had to take a lot of trouble diversifying our Accra staff, or otherwise it would have been pure Ewe. When we started up there were thirteen newspapers in Accra, all of which we ultimately put out of business, partly by publishing more news, and no political abuse, and partly because of our delivery arrangements.

When we began, Nkrumah was the editor and Gbedemah the manager of the Accra *Evening News*. It was a propaganda sheet pure and simple. I first met Nkrumah to sell him a second-hand printing press, but over the years I saw quite a lot of him on my brief visits. He is an attractive man to meet, with considerable charm. He must have been a great rabble-rouser, though I never heard him deliver a political speech. He was very insistent on being called Dr Nkrumah, though the doctorate was only honorary and from a third-rate American university. He had no great gifts, but happened to be the leader of the Nationalist Party at a time when self-government was imminent. His predecessor, Dr Danquah, was an educated man and a much more considerable character. He was so confident of becoming Prime Minister of a self-governing Gold Coast that he was said to have parted with his wife in order to acquire one more in keeping with his future status. He was also said to have sent this lady to England to be trained in her new duties. Anyway, when I met him his envy, hatred and jealousy of Nkrumah was crashingly obvious. The Governor of the Gold Coast in my day was Arden-Clark, I suppose the best of the West Coast Governors of that period. He was not a good administrator, but had a good political sense, which was more necessary. His mistake was to build up only Nkrumah, and this paved the way to dictatorship.

The trouble with Nkrumah was that he was a good politician and evidently an excellent speaker, but he had no administrative ability and could not be made to understand finance. Arden-

157

Clark very properly tried to convince him that when you reach the top you must kick away some of the ladders by which you rose, and bring into your inner circle others who had opposed you hitherto. Without the educated minority, however contemptuous and unhelpful they might have been, it would be impossible to govern the country. To this unanswerable argument Nkrumah made no response at all and continued to antagonize the judges, senior civil servants and chiefs, while surrounding himself with 'verandah boys'. A further factor in Nkrumah's downfall was that he aspired to be the leading figure in black Africa. It is probably much too early for any such figure, but it could only be achieved by good government at home and good relations with Ghana's immediate neighbours. But Ghana was badly misgoverned, and his relations with Togo and the Ivory Coast could not have been worse. He finally took to financing subversive activities against self-governing African states even further afield, for instance Sierra Leone, and his relations with Nigeria, much the most important of all black African States, were consistently bad. So the money spent in bringing 'socialism' to Africa merely made enemies. In any case 'socialism' was merely a word for speeches, and though taken seriously by some left-wing people in England, mainly served to conceal a personal dictatorship of the South American banana republic type. Nkrumah was no organizer, and in fact the vital victory at the polls was won while he was in prison. In one of the most ungenerous autobiographies ever written, he made no mention of the debt he owed to Gbedemah and his very great organizing abilities.

The policy of the Ghana *Graphic* was the same as that of the Nigerian *Daily Times*, to keep the political temperature low, to encourage the advance of self-government, to keep reports of crime to a minimum, and give all the information about world markets in cocoa and timber etc. that would enable the Ghanaians to see what was going on in the world that would affect their economy. In all this, the papers on the Coast were greatly helped by *West Africa* and its editor, David Williams, who knew more about what was happening in West Africa, at all levels, than anyone past or present. *West Africa* had been an influential paper in the thirties, owned and edited by one Cartwright, but by the time we bought it the sale was down to 850, and there was evidence that most of these copies were not read. However, under Williams's editorship it has become easily the leading magazine of its kind in the world, with subscribers (several!) in both the State Department and the Kremlin. Now, with a sale of 20,000, it has become a leading source of information for Africans about Africa. In particular it was *West Africa* that led the way in interesting Anglophone West Africa in its Francophone neighbours, and now, though concentrating on West Africa, is a mine of information about other parts of black Africa.

When we began operations in Ghana the existing press was quite rightly alarmed. It did nothing to improve its coverage or distribution, but launched a violent campaign against me. 'Away White Press', 'Go Home Mr King', I remember, were slogans in frequent use. I was even described as an 'Imperialist Serpent', which seemed inappropriate in view of my size and bulk. Eventually we sold the *Graphic* to the Government, not because of political difficulties, but because the incompetence of the exchange and import control system was gradually bringing us to a halt. I suppose our total investment in West Africa was about £600,000. We got this back and more, and now have a half-interest in the large and profitable Nigerian business for nothing.

As we were in possession of two flourishing businesses in Nigeria and the Gold Coast, it seemed logical to have one in Sierra Leone, which we decided to do in 1952. We bought the *Daily Mail* from its African owners and imagined we should have no difficulty in collecting and training a competent staff. Had not Freetown been called the 'Athens of West Africa', supplying lawyers and administrators for the whole West Coast? However that may have been in the last century, in the mid-twentieth the position was quite different. We never succeeded in collecting an adequate staff, and most competent members were either Nigerians or Ghanaians. Whatever had happened to the intelligent and cultured Creoles of the last century, we never learned. Any survivors in my day were very old, like Mrs Casely-Hayford, who must have been over eighty. Apart from the difficulty of finding staff of any competence at any level, there were the inherent difficulties of the terrain. Freetown and the Colony are on a rocky peninsula, mountainous in the centre and quite well populated round the edge. But once you leave the peninsula there are fifty miles or more, thinly inhabited by poor and illiterate villagers before you come to Bo, which is more of a large village than a town. Eventually we sold the paper at a loss to the Sierra Leone Government. It was a disappointing venture which took up far more time of myself and others than it ever could have been worth.

The two leading politicians in my day were Siaka Stevens and Milton Margai. The former was a trade union leader, the latter a doctor by profession. Siaka Stevens was able, but only recently managed to form a Government. Milton Margai was no ball of fire but was, I suppose, adequate, only he lingered on long after he was past it. His brother Albert Margai succeeded him, and I thought he would prove much better, but not so, he got his country into such a mess that he had to be deposed. By far the ablest Sierra Leonian was Dr Davidson Nicol, who gave up a fellowship at Cambridge to be the head of Fourah Bay College, but has now left the country, one would suppose fed up with the antics of its rulers.

During the period when I became interested in Sierra Leone, the most fascinating development was the illicit diamond digging and smuggling. When I first arrived the Governor was Beresford-Stooke, a rather eccentric type who traversed vast areas of his colony on foot. Though not fully appreciated in Whitehall, he was an excellent Governor for Sierra Leone. He was succeeded by one de Zouche Hall, under whom the diamond problem came to a head. David Williams found on one of his periodic visits that the Selection Trust's concession to mine was being extensively infringed and that a million pounds a year in diamonds was being smuggled abroad with no benefit to Sierra Leone. This was really quite a story, which he sent to the *Financial Times*, but they did not even acknowledge it! The next year the figure had risen to four million, but the Government would only admit to one million. The next year the figure was believed to be twelve million, and the Government put it at not more than four. The Diamond Corporation were brought in to stop the smuggling by offering full market prices. They put the figure of illicit digging at six million when it was far more, as was easily ascertained by asking the banks in Freetown, by asking the airline pilots in Monrovia how often they flew out parcels of diamonds and by enquiring in Antwerp what was the value of Sierra Leone diamonds sent for cutting. For years we knew the figure to be far larger than was realized by the Selection Trust, the Colonial Government or the Diamond Corporation. This was only a subject of minor interest to us, but to the economy of Sierra Leone this was the most important matter. Apart from anything else, the number of Africans who took part in the illicit digging was so large that the colony was unable to feed itself and had to import large amounts of rice.

When I was in the diamond country, I was told of a lady who thought one of the stones in her drive was a diamond. She encountered a good deal of scepticism, but she was eventually proved right and sold her diamond to a Lebanese trader for £30,000. Her husband suggested that the sum was so large it should be entrusted to him for investment. However, the next thing that happened was that her husband departed to Liberia with a girl friend and the £30,000! There should be a moral in this, but I am not sure what!

For sixteen years I was a frequent visitor to some part or other of West Africa with visits of about three weeks every eight months. During that period I paid brief visits to most of Nigeria, Ghana and Sierra Leone and to parts of Dahomey, the Cameroons, Togo, Liberia, Gambia and Senegal. During those years I met everyone of importance in the former British colonies, and also saw something of Mr Sekou Touré of French Guinea. The Africans are desperately keen to learn and respect anyone who can teach them anything. So while the British colonial civil servant had little prestige, because he had no specialized knowledge, the experts in agriculture or (in my case) newspaper publishing and general printing, were really listened to. And once you had established the fact that you were really training the African staff to take over the top management, their co-operation was a hundred per cent. It was curious that when we handed over the management of the *Daily Graphic* to the African staff, we were much criticized by the managers of other European-owned firms for selling the pass. Actually such a development was long overdue, and we should have arrived at that point years earlier if we had arrived in the Gold Coast sooner. The African staff were fully competent and have run the company with great success since our departure.

Any idea that Africans are stupid or incompetent is nonsense, as one soon learns if one employs many hundreds as we still do. In any case, men such as Professor Dike and Dr Biobaku would hold their own on sheer intelligence in any company in the world. Africans are not Europeans, and have until recently been living in villages a life rather similar to ours of some centuries ago. But even so, we trained good newspaper stereo-typers in ten weeks, straight from the bush, while in England it is a five-year apprenticeship. Even process blockmakers only took ten months to train. Africans are not Europeans with black faces, but it is hard to disentangle the differences due to environment from those due to heredity. To begin with, they have immense vitality. So often Africans accused of laziness are sustaining a menagerie of internal parasites that would kill an Englishman. They are warmer, more emotional, more telepathic, more personal. They seem to be more musical; they certainly have a better sense of rhythm, but find our impersonal, mathematical, computerized world harder to understand than we do. Looking out on the contemporary world, an Englishman can see all around him developments

162

from postage stamps to jet engines that owed their origin to our countrymen. But an African doing the same thing sees nothing that was created or started by an African, and is bound therefore to have some feeling of inferiority. Jazz music and dancing and an influence on some modern sculpture is the most that can be attributed to Africa. What they have got, and this is also true of the Negroes in America, is a far greater degree of happiness. You hardly ever hear a child cry in West Africa. They are a happy people and often a wise people, and what we all want is happiness and wisdom rather than cleverness and wealth.

African women are in general in a state of subjection to their men, but that does not prevent women becoming the big traders. Mrs Nzimero of Port Harcourt had her agents in every market for forty miles around, and kept no books, but knew from day to day exactly where she stood. From her account with the United Africa Company one could calculate that her profit must have been of the order of £50,000 per annum – and that with little or no taxes to pay. Madame Pobi of Cape Castle was believed to net quite £10,000 a year, but was usually to be seen in her shop selling many things, including our papers. These women were at the top of their profession, but in many towns the market women were a political and economic force to be reckoned with.

Over the years our papers acquired a terrific reputation for reliability, and in the recent troubles in Nigeria, with official radio bulletins from different centres telling very different stories, it was the *Daily Times* to which the Nigerian public turned, and the same was true of the *Daily Graphic* in Ghana. Both these papers became national institutions of some stability in a rapidly changing society; at times in Nigeria the only stable national institution. It was curious that though this was true, visiting newspapermen from England or elsewhere hardly ever called on our people for help, which they would have been given very willingly. Much nonsense from West Africa would never have been published, had this help been sought.

When working in a market like West Africa, one gets an

impression of the export efforts made by different countries and firms. While naturally biased in favour of British firms, we found ourselves buying German, Swedish and Italian printing presses, French tyres and, in fact, surprisingly little from home. Many of the trading firms on the spot were British, but management in general was sluggish, the bright exceptions being Shell and Barclays Bank. The civil engineering contracts mostly went to Italian firms, and they gave the various governments excellent service.

India

In 1947 Mr Munshi, Leader of the Bombay Bar and at one time Home Member of the Bombay Government, was contemplating publishing a newspaper, and invited Bartholomew to send someone out to Bombay to discuss the technical aspects of such a paper – and I was sent. When I got to Bombay and met Mr Munshi, I discovered the paper had been launched or was being launched (I never discovered which) and there was really nothing for me to do. The paper had been planned with purely political motives and was the failure one would expect. However, I was not discouraged as I wanted to get to India to meet Mr Gandhi, and also see something of the country in which my father and grandfather had spent so much of their lives. To this end I had introductions from Stafford Cripps and Pethick Lawrence, then Secretary of State for India. So from Bombay I went to Delhi to meet Mr Gandhi and his circle. It had always been said in England that Gandhi had been financed by rich Indians for their own reasons, but this was certainly not the attitude of Mr Munshi and later of Mr Birla, with whom I spent much of my time in Delhi. In fact it was one aspect of the greatness of Gandhi that while the simplest villagers regarded him as the reincarnation of the God Rama and were prepared to do more about child marriages and untouchability at his request than had been done by everyone put together in centuries, he had also the entire loyalty and devotion of the highly educated and the very rich. Mr Munshi told me he felt greatly honoured when asked by Gandhi for a large cheque.

165

It would be unthinkable for him to ask what it was for!

Mr Birla was, and doubtless still is, an immensely wealthy industrialist. I saw none of his enterprises but seem to remember his main interests were cotton and jute. He was one of the main, if not the main financier behind Gandhi. The other leading figures at that time were Patel, who was the organizer and administrator, and Nehru who was regarded as the orator and less important than the other two. In fact he was regarded as a bit of a windbag. I had lunch alone with him and his daughter, now Prime Minister of India. In their turn they have ruled in India not because of their capacity, but because through the death of Patel the mantle of the great Gandhi has fallen on them. I spent a morning with Jinnah to hear about his plans for Pakistan. At that time it seemed unthinkable that India would be divided. I thought him most unattractive and a man of immense personal ambition. He was not interested in the welfare of his Moslem brethren, he was interested in Jinnah. He couldn't rule India so he would settle for Pakistan, and would wade through blood to get what he wanted.

I had lunch with the Viceroy, Lord Wavell. Here is a note I made at the time.

'The guests collected in the ADCs' room and drank cocktails until one o'clock arrived. 'Chips' Channon, MP for Southend, had arrived by air that morning with a friend and was staying: another guest was an American colonel who had been tiger-shooting at Jaipur with one of the ADCs. At one we were ushered into the drawing-room where two young women of the household introduced us to an Indian and his wife, who were also guests for lunch. Presently we were drawn up in a line, the Viceroy and Lady Wavell came in, and we were introduced by the senior ADC – and so into lunch, where I sat between the ADC and one of the ladies-in-waiting. The ADC was very chatty – the only point he made of any consequence was that the Muslim League was a really constructive body – quite different from the Congress people. After lunch we went back to the drawing-room where I amused myself going through the papers on the table to see what was read in the Vice-regal Lodge. Prominent were *The Times*, the *Spectator*, the *Observer*, *Punch* and *Country Life*. The only publication which could by any stretch of the imagination be called progressive was one copy of the *New Statesman* buried under a pile of more reactionary journals. Presently I was taken by the ADC to sit on a sofa with the Vicereine. We had some uninteresting talk, except that she, too, said how far more statesmanlike and constructive were the Muslims compared with the Congress people. Later, I was wafted away to talk to the Viceroy. He is a most charming person – looking older and more worried than when I saw him last about four years ago. He is a charming Colonel Blimp – can have very little idea of what modern politics are all about – his mind is stuck somewhere around 1910 – but he is an entirely honest man anxious to do anything possible for his country and for India. We talked for about twenty minutes about this and that, but only two points emerged of any interest:

1. He also said how far more constructive and well-intentioned the Muslims were than the Congress people, and
2. When asked whether in his view our army should leave India, he declined to give an opinion – though I made it quite clear that I realized this is a political decision to be made by the Cabinet in London, and that I should treat anything he said in confidence. It seemed – and seems – to me that he should maintain the strictest neutrality on the Communal issues in India – which he didn't, but that he should have been more helpful on the question of whether or not our Army should leave India on an early date – a subject on which the Congress leaders are very vocal.'

His whole attitude seemed to me incomprehensible. A campaign in the *Mirror* at that time to bring our troops back

from India would have been effective, and there I could reasonably expect to have his views. The crucial problem before the
country, then and since, lay in the relations between the Moslems and Hindus, and on this any Viceroy of any discretion
at all could only assume an attitude of complete impartiality
whatever his private thoughts might be. The people round
Gandhi were very fair about this. They saw why the public
school type could get on with Moslems and yet be completely
baffled by Hindus. This largely social point had the inevitable
effect of making us more favourable to the Moslem minority
than to the Hindu majority. But even if this was inevitable to
some extent, there was no reason why it should be carried to
the point shown by Wavell and his entourage.

'When in Calcutta I was invited to lunch by Sir Frederick
Burrows, Governor of Bengal. He was at one time president
of the NUR and his appointment had caused some surprise
at the time. From the view I had heard expressed of him
in India I didn't know what to expect. To meet he is a
bluff hearty Englishman – just the type you would think to
handle the tortuous Bengali. He obviously hates the place –
at one time he said he had been in Calcutta eight months
– "Nine months" said his wife – "It feels like nine years."
Without any experience at all of any remotely similar problem, he is pitchforked into running a vast province – I think
as big as France and Germany, with a huge population, poor
communications, acute communal tension (the population is
about forty-six per cent Hindu, who have all the money and
fifty-four per cent Muslim) and conditions of near famine.
During his short term of office there have been bad riots in
Calcutta, with perhaps five thousand killed and bad riots in
Eastern Bengal, where the casualties have been lower, but still
serious. In both affairs Burrows has been blamed for not
acting more quickly and taking the situation in hand, as he
has the power to do under the Act of 1935. His reply is that
in a desperately poor province where there are the poorest

168

Cecil King as Chairman of the Reed Paper Group surrounded by members of the staff at the opening of the Killingworth factory of Reed Cartons.

154. Cecil King being received by President Johnson in his tiny, heavily-curtained sitting-room in the White House. On his left is Ralph Champion, head of the *Daily Mirror* New York Bureau. Opposite sits Mr

communications – mostly by boat (and most boats were destroyed at the time of the threatened Japanese invasion), and hardly any police, it is almost impossible to avoid trouble. The police in some areas average about twenty-five men – and these all natives – to an area the size of an English county. The Noakhale disturbances were apparently organized – not, he thought, by Jinnah – but by some local Muslim politician or some local thug who chose an area so remote that it was a week or more before news of the disturbances reached Calcutta. Burrows's view, both over this and over the Calcutta trouble was that the Provincial Government – a Muslim League affair – should have time to show what it could do and only in the event of a total breakdown should the Governor intervene. This view is supported by the Government at home and seems sound. But the universal view in India is that, even so, he was far too slow. This view was echoed by his predecessor, Casey, whom I met in Melbourne. A factor which may have complicated matters is that Wavell and Burrows obviously have nothing in common – whereas Wavell and Nye (at Madras), both professional soldiers, are generally believed in India to be great friends. My own feeling is that while opinion in India may be too hard on Burrows, his superiors at home apparently continue to believe him a success.'

While I was with Burrows he showed me round the State Apartments, including the Ballroom. I was amused to see thrones at each end. Burrows explained that the Governor of Bengal represented the King, so did the Viceroy. When they were both present, as sometimes occurred before the capital moved to Delhi, they were both entitled to thrones!

Finally it was arranged that I should see Gandhi at his *ashram* one evening. We had an appointment, but there was a meeting of the Congress Party's controlling Committee and I had to wait outside until this meeting broke up. I remember sitting or lying on a charpoy, the Indian string bed, wondering when the

M
169

meeting would be over. However, it did end, and my companion Bill Berbert and I were ushered into the presence. To me
Gandhi was a very unimpressive man to meet, small, ugly and
insignificant. On his record, he must be one of the half-dozen
greatest men of my lifetime, but I could not see it or feel it when
in his presence – and I came to admire, not to scoff. He sat on a
sort of wooden shelf with a secretary each side of him. My
companion and I sat on bolsters on the floor. It intrigued me
that everything he said was taken down by his secretaries but
nothing I said, which must have made the transcript a bit one-
sided! I asked him if he thought Hinduism had the answer to the
spiritual problems of the world. He said, no. I got the impression
he thought Hinduism too old, too adulterated, too corrupt to
hold the twentieth century. I asked where we could look for
help. He said it was right for me to seek a logical answer, but this
was not right for him, he must seek a miracle. I asked him if
he had experienced any miracles and he said, yes: two. The first
was when the British, after winning the South African war,
gave self-government to South Africa in 1909; the other was
when Churchill, the great enemy of Indian self-government was
rejected at the polls in 1945. Another remark of his that impressed me was that he said India should always be grateful to
England for two things, introducing the English language and
building the Indian railways, the two binding forces that would
keep India together.

From Delhi I went to Agra, Benares and Calcutta. The filth
and poverty of Calcutta are appalling. I regard it as one of the
two most depressing cities I have ever visited; the other for very
different reasons being Johannesburg. But the Fort at Agra is
enchanting, with channels running through the royal apartments
with water brought by canal from seventy miles away, and
written round the cornice in black marble on white, 'If there
is a paradise on earth, it is this, it is this, it is this.' And the Taj
– one of the authentic wonders of the world. However many
pictures you may have seen, the Taj Mahal is a miracle of
beauty. People have said, 'See Naples and die', when the Bay

of Naples is no lovelier than Dublin Bay and not as lovely as the Bay of Hobart in Tasmania. But the Taj is like the Acropolis, an immense achievement of the human spirit.

I continued my spiritual pilgrimage in India by going on to Benares, the Rome of Hinduism. But it is not an inspiring experience. The cremations by the water-side, the hordes of crippled beggars, the crows picking at corpses or parts of corpses floating down the river have a depressing effect that even the fervour of the crowds cannot dispel. In any case crowds of women bathing in the sacred river in *saris*, of all unsuitable garments for bathing, leave an impression mainly of squalor.

Since 1946 I have paid two visits to India, once to examine the possibilities of buying the *Statesman*, then owned by Miss Yule, and more recently when I spent two weeks in South India as the guest of the Indian Government. I was particularly keen to visit the Hindu temples, and most of the great ones are in the South, so I visited Bombay again, Madras, Bangalore, Mysore, Madura. Though the Indians are a deeply spiritual people, the impression of Hinduism in the temples has become so conventionalized as to be quite meaningless. In fact it seemed to me that the atmosphere was, if anything, evil.

The Chief Minister of Mysore was very friendly and told me that the esteem in which Englishmen were held had never been higher. I was amused to see that the big clock over the market in Bangalore was out of order and someone had pasted across the face a piece of paper with the word 'Sick'.

An amusing incident of an earlier visit to India was queuing up for a ticket at a Bombay cinema. While I stood in line, a little man with two friends went to the head of the queue and started buying tickets. This outraged my sense of fairness, so I picked the little man up and dumped him at the end of the queue to the delight of the crowd. When I had bought my ticket I heard he was the cinema manager. However, he stayed where I put him until I had gone.

Bombay is the centre of the very large motion picture industry of India, larger than the Japanese and only smaller than the American. The films tend to be too long for European taste. The music is unintelligible to our ears and the love-making is too discreet. Lovers may only goggle to each other; no contact is admissible.

The most memorable part of my visit to an Indian film studio was meeting the famous elephant Shantaram. He is an immensely popular film star because he is the only elephant that can dance in time to music. Apart from this unexpected talent, he is a most lovable beast, with a taste for coconuts which he cracks gently with his foot.

I am afraid the main impression left on me by India is that of appalling, hopeless poverty. In West Africa there are millions of people with no possessions, but they have enough or nearly enough to eat. In India everywhere there are crowds of starving people, grey with hunger; children with swollen bellies and stick-like legs, constituting a problem of baffling magnitude.

It would be nice to think India is making a success of self-government but it clearly is not. With all the help it receives from the West it is not holding its own even in comparison with China. It has been said that India is incapable of self-government and has in fact been governed by foreigners since the reign of Asoka in the fifth century. Though this sounds unduly pessimistic, they are certainly doing very badly, even after full allowance is made for the population explosion which always overtakes any increase in the food supply.

Australasia

The firm's excursion into Australia had the same cause as our investment in Nigeria; there was no chance of expansion in the newspaper field in the UK because of newsprint rationing, if for no other reason, so expansion overseas was the only way out.

In the later forties Bart heard that the Americans were negotiating with Ezra Norton for the purchase of his newspaper *Truth*, a rather lurid Sunday paper that was published all over Australia and in New Zealand, and the Sydney *Daily Mirror*, an evening paper. Bart thought the Australian *Daily Mirror* should not fall into alien hands: we knew as much about newspaper publishing as the Americans, so why not have a go? So although he was no negotiator, he went out to Australia to forestall the Americans. Ezra Norton was a difficult man at any time, but as a negotiator he must have been a problem. Eventually, it was clear he had decided not to sell. These bouts of negotiations recurred from time to time. He was a sick man: he was attracted by the idea of a big price, but then reflected that, as it was, he was a big man on the Australian scene, but without his newspapers he would be a rich man, but not one who would enjoy either respect or influence. It was many years before he finally sold out to Rupert Murdoch, now one of the leading publishers in Australia.

But to return to Bart. Having been frustrated in his aim to buy the Sydney *Daily Mirror*, he became bitten with the idea of buying an Australian paper and the only one that might be available was the Melbourne *Argus* – once one of the great

173

newspapers of the world, but by this time in rather low water. Eventually a successful, but extravagant bid was made for the shares, and we took over the joint management with Sir Erroll Knox, the managing director. Though the *Argus* had been a great newspaper and a profitable one, it had made the cardinal error of discarding the small classified advertisements during the War. So we were confronted in Melbourne with the *Sun Pictorial*, which had much the biggest sale and was excellently managed by Sir Keith Murdoch, and the *Age*, under the conservative management and ownership of the Syme family, by whom it had been founded a century earlier. Their newspaper had the bulk of the classified advertisements which bring not only revenue but readers. Erroll Knox's secret weapon was to install presses that would print colour. The plant consisted of offset colour presses feeding into ordinary letter-press machinery. This was expensive and an almighty gamble. No one knew whether such a set-up in the press-room would work, or what would be the demand for colour from readers or from advertisers. In the outcome, after endless headaches for the production people, the colour wasn't bad, but its impact on the public was less than had been hoped for. On a big day, like the Queen's visit or the Melbourne Cup, our colour sold newspapers but on ordinary days it did not, and colour in the paper delayed the production at night and usually the time was more valuable than the colour. Some advertisers came into the paper because of the colour, but not enough to affect the fortunes of the paper. The *Age* had three commercial radio stations in country districts, and these were helpful to the newspaper as well as profitable in themselves. Looking back, I think we were trying the impossible. There was only room for two morning papers in Melbourne, and by the time we arrived those two were clearly to be the *Sun Pictorial* and the *Age*. By the end under the leadership of John Patience and Alex McKay, we were producing an excellent paper, but as we learned later at home with the *Sun*, if there is no room for a paper, there is no room, and editorial excellence will not alter this. Much was made of the fact that when we took over, the politics of the paper were changed from extreme Conservatism to Labour. This may well have upset some of the advertisers, but as far as my observations went, this had no fatal long term effect.

As time went on, Bart became rather bitten with Australia, and when we were offered the controlling interest in a chain of radio stations, including 2 GB, the principal commercial radio station in Sydney, he was determined to go ahead. This was a very profitable deal indeed, but we were not to know how profitable for some years. In the meantime the finances of the *Argus* venture were looking increasingly ominous. I judged we had irrevocably lost a million, would probably lose a second million and might well lose a third. It was because of this that I decided to try and remove Bartholomew from the chairmanship. This would have been easier had I not been the inevitable successor. However, Bartholomew was called on to resign, and for the first three years as the new chairman, my principal worry was Australia. In the end we sold the *Argus* to the Melbourne *Herald* and the radio stations to Associated Television, who in their turn sold at a good profit. We scrambled out of our Australian episode with a total capital profit of £80,000, having of course had no return on our Australian investment during the years we were seeking to establish ourselves.

My own first visit had been to Australia from India in 1946 in a flying boat – Calcutta, Rangoon, Surabaja to Bowen in North Queensland and so to Sydney. These flying boats were roomy and comfortable, though by modern standards slow, and of course by flying much lower than planes do nowadays much more subject to the buffetings of the weather. I remember saying to the pilot that it was comforting being in a flying boat, so much safer than a plane over the sea. He said, 'Not so, you cannot be sure when you're taking off there is no submerged log on the runway. Sooner or later there is bound to be one which will tear the bottom out of any flying boat.' We had flown over the Timor Sea by night, a very rough night indeed. In the morning the pilot asked me if I had noticed a big bump in which we had risen three thousand feet in a few seconds, and all four engines had cut out! Mercifully I had not particularly noticed this event. I was probably too punch-drunk to care.

My first view of Australia was Bowen, a small sugar port in Northern Queensland, at 6.30 a.m. The passengers all made a bee-line for the lavatory, which was out of order. However, the bar was open. Licensing hours were 6 a.m. to 6 p.m., and two local characters were enjoying their whiskies even at that early hour.

I was sent to Australia to see what could be done about syndicating *Mirror* material in the Australian Press, but I liked travel and was also concerned with seeing something of Australia. One of my recollections of that visit is of having supper in a Chinese restaurant in Sydney. The radio was switched on and the programme proved to be the London *Daily Mirror's* talking dog. A reader had written in to say he had a dog which said 'I want one' when he wanted a drink of beer. Indeed the noise the dog made could plausibly be interpreted as 'I want one': and here we were fourteen thousand miles away having the *Mirror* dog on the radio.

One of my most vivid memories of that visit to Australia is of driving for hours and miles through the Australian bush and of suddenly arriving at a large building in the dark. It was the Parliament Building and we were in Canberra, at that time a small place and so spread out as to be hardly perceptible. I met Chifley, the Prime Minister, next day. Though he had not the gifts, intellectual or other, of either Evatt or Menzies, he was a better party leader than Evatt: a better Prime Minister than Menzies. I spent a week-end on a sheep farm at Yass, not far from Canberra, and so had my first taste of the glorious Australian countryside. Though my hosts had ten thousand sheep and must have been wealthy, they all worked exceedingly hard. The daughter helped the father, and a hired man looked after the sheep, while mother and a friend ran the house. It would not be possible to keep so many sheep on such a small staff in England because our sheep are far more prone to parasites and pests of all kinds, but in Australia it could be done, though only by long hours of strenuous work.

The strongest memory of that visit was perhaps the appalling quality of Australian hotels. They are nothing special now, but show a dramatic improvement on what they were twenty years ago. The second impression was the gigantic chip Australians carried on their shoulders. Almost any remark, however innocuous, was apt to be interpreted as a slight. This was carried to such extreme lengths that it was apt to get Englishmen down if they had to work there. Why Australians should have had such an inferiority complex is hard to say. Mercifully it has now all but gone, though they are still, rather inexplicably, touchy at any mention of convicts or Botany Bay.

My next visit was five years later when I had become chairman of the *Mirror* group and was there to see on the spot what should be done about the *Argus* and all that. As I have said earlier, we had bought a controlling interest in a string of commercial radio stations centred on 2 GB Sydney. Naturally we had not made the purchase without ascertaining from the appropriate official that the Australian Government had no objection to our purchase. What was our amazement therefore when the Postmaster General, Mr Anthony, got up in the House and said that a foreign group had surreptitiously bought a controlling interest in an important group of Australian radio stations. Much indignation was expressed and resolutions were passed through both Houses censuring the transaction. The following day our solicitor called on the Postmaster General with the letter from the Australian Broadcasting Control Board, saying the Government had no objection to the purchase. It then appeared that the official who signed the letter had not told his Minister. We never learned the reason for this extraordinary behaviour. The official concerned retired, but we were stuck with the Parliamentary resolutions. We satisfied the Postmaster General by the sale of some shares to the *Sydney*

Morning Herald, but these resolutions dogged us later when we wanted a serious share in Australian television. I think the total foreign share was limited to twenty-five per cent of any television company, and the share of any one foreigner to twenty per cent, which constitutes an investment, not a partnership as was intended.

I suppose since 1951 I have visited Australia half a dozen times, at first to keep an eye on the operation of the *Argus* and of 2 GB, subsequently to watch the build-up of the Reed Paper Group's interests. In the course of my various visits I have seen the Australian coast most of the way round from Bowen in Queensland to Dampier in northern West Australia, that is, part of Southern Queensland, most of New South Wales, all Victoria, a lot of South Australia, West Australia from Albany to Dampier, and Tasmania. This is, of course, far more than ninety-nine per cent of Australians have seen of their country. Most Australians live in the six capital cities, which are undistinguished. Melbourne, the former capital of the Commonwealth, has an air about it, though no natural advantages.

Sydney is built on the most wonderful site in the world, of which the city fathers have made nothing. But Australian countryside is one of the wonders of the world, totally unlike any other. To begin with, the light is quite different. I am not susceptible to qualities of light, but in Australia, as in Greece, light has a quality all its own that one just cannot miss. Of course Australia is a vast country and the space is immensely impressive, and the colouring is unique. The trees are mostly eucalyptus, of which there are hundreds of varieties, and eucalyptus is an evergreen. The leaves of almost all kinds of eucalyptus are exactly alike, so the trees are named after their bark, iron-bark, stringy-bark and so on. The soil, particularly in the drier parts, is often red and sometimes a blinding scarlet. The weather is violent, with no rain for two years and then inches in minutes. The climate is so different from the English one, except perhaps in Tasmania, that it must in time bring about a difference in the national temperament. As it is, the Australian temperament is far more Irish than one would expect. About a quarter of the population is Catholic and, except for the more recent Italian intake, Catholic means Irish. In Ireland the men tend to drink too much and are prone to fight. The sexual element in Australian society is very different from that in America or Canada. It is a very noticeable contrast coming from Vancouver to Sydney. In British Columbia you sell even machine tools by showing a buxom young woman drooping her breasts over the machine. In Australia, at any rate until recently, this element was largely absent. Perhaps as part of the same attitude, while Australian men are the handsomest in the world, their womenfolk would not rate high in any international beauty rating.

Naturally I have seen much of the newspaper editors, managers and proprietors, a most colourful band of buccaneers. The biggest and the ablest was Sir Keith Murdoch, who had built up the Melbourne *Herald* group from nothing. He had been given his start by Northcliffe when he was a reporter in Gallipoli. Not only had Northcliffe publicly praised his work, he had helped him with money when he wanted to launch out on his own. Though this was nearly forty years earlier, Keith always gratefully remembered how much he owed to my family. His wife Dame Elizabeth is one of the nicest and most respected women in Australia, and must have been a great help to him. Keith himself used to put on an act as an 'English gentleman of the old school' and used a top hat to an un-Australian extent to drive home the point. If anyone were foolish enough to take this pose seriously and to lower his guard, he would swiftly be disillusioned.

The second of the big publishers was Frank Packer. He had come of a newspaper family – his father was an editor – but at the early age of seventeen he had launched out on his own and, with partners, had found a gold mine in Fiji. With this money he had started the exceedingly successful *Australian Woman's Weekly* and subsequently had acquired the Sydney *Daily*

Telegraph. He is more of a magazine man than a newspaper man and is now deep in television. He had been amateur heavyweight boxing champion of Australia. When I first met him he shook me firmly by the hand and said, 'I am interested in girls and horses, what are you interested in?' My Wykehamist upbringing had not allowed for such an introduction, and my response must have been disappointing. Frank has always been pleasant to me and I regard him as one of the attractively colourful characters of my acquaintance.

When I arrived on the scene Ezra Norton was the proprietor of *Truth* and the Sydney *Daily Mirror*. No one could call him an attractive figure, though he was an astute publisher, as they all were. Feelings between him and Packer were rather strained, as there had been an episode at the races when one of Norton's men held Packer while Norton is said to have leapt on his back and bitten him in the face. My clearest recollection of Norton is of having lunch with him at the Malmaison, the smartest lunch place in Sydney at that time. Norton, looking sour and ill, discoursed on his piles.

John Coope, one of my colleagues on the *Mirror* board, was told a story of his racing by Ezra Norton. He had had a bad day – he had lost £7,000 and there was only one race left. But he had an idea; a jockey he knew had a good mount and might win, so he sent for the jockey and asked if he could win. He said he thought he could, but had orders not to. Ezra said he would put £1,000 on for the jockey's benefit for a win. The jockey said he would do his best, and he won. And that is how, according to Ezra, he turned a very bad day's racing into a very good one, repaying himself the jockey's £1,000 and his own losses and leaving a handsome margin.

Next to the Melbourne *Herald* group in importance was the *Sydney Morning Herald* controlled by Warwick Fairfax, a retiring figure of whom I saw little, but managed by Rupert Henderson, whose character was quite as vivid as that of the proprietors I have mentioned.

Though these men were mainly concerned in publishing their

papers and most of them in doing each other down, their papers were good. Perhaps I am prejudiced but, certainly in the popular field, I would put the British Press first, followed by the Australian. I do not think the American, Canadian, South African or Continental European newspapers are nearly so good.

During most of my visits to Australia the Prime Minister was Mr Menzies and the leader of the Labour Opposition was Dr Evatt. They were both sons of country store-keepers and intellectually towered over their contemporaries. Evatt's deputy was a genial Irishman called Calwell and Menzies' crown prince was a pleasant nonentity called Holt. Calwell was for a time a hopelessly ineffective Leader of the Opposition and Holt, before his tragic death, was an equally colourless Prime Minister. Though Menzies had so many gifts, of intellect, charm and eloquence, he was not a great Prime Minister, and Australia forged ahead with little help from Bob. Holt was the sort of crown prince who would never shorten Bob's reign. Evatt was not a politician and was desperate to be Prime Minister. In the outcome he never made it, and split his party in the process. I have never met Gorton the present Prime Minister, but suspect he will be no match for Whitlam, the new and relatively young Labour leader.

Australia in the long run has alarming problems. How do you keep the country more or less empty with hundreds of millions of hungry Asiatics looking in from the north? In the shorter run, Australia offers a future similar to the American West in the last century. This is particularly true of West Australia, which is fortunate to have in Charles Court, the development Minister, the outstanding political figure I met in all my Australian visits. It is his energy and enthusiasm that has brought about the development of iron-ore mining in the north of his State, nickel-mining near Kalgoorlie, oil on Barrow Island and the breaking up annually of a million acres of bush to be turned into good wheat land. Similar possibilities may well exist in other parts of Australia but they are not being developed with the same drive. Though Western Australia has hit the headlines most in recent years, the biggest single development is the Snowy River scheme on the border between Victoria and New South Wales. All in all, Australia is an immensely exciting country even to visit. The whole vast island or continent is being transformed, while here we wrangle for years before building a few miles of new motorway.

Though it is now so many years since we pulled out of Australia, there is still a reminder of the influence we had. Sir Henry Bolte was then the leader of a small group in the Victorian House, but became Premier of his State thanks to a campaign in his favour in the *Argus*. He has been a great success and is still Premier of his State thirteen years later.

I have been twice to New Zealand, once more than twelve years ago and once more recently. Before visiting the country one tends to wonder why there is such antagonism between the New Zealanders and the Australians. They are both pioneering communities of similar stock. Surely they must be very similar people. Actually, the difference between the two people is much greater than anyone would expect. Australia is a brash young country roaring ahead: New Zealand is ethnically more British, but very hidebound, very set in its ways. I remember talking to the Professor of Geology at Canberra University, who said, 'The trouble with New Zealand is that it has been cut off from the rest of the world for 250 million years.' The first time I visited the country, the evening meal in the hotels was served from 6 to 7. If you arrived at 6.50 you had ten minutes to eat your meal. If you arrived at 7.10 you would be developing a fine appetite by breakfast!

It is a most beautiful country. The North Island is lovely: the South Island even more so. The scenery is now rather odd, a mixture of Scottish trees and bushes, animals and birds, and the indigenous. So you drive along a road which might well be in Scotland, turn a corner and find yourself in a thicket of tree ferns. When Captain Cook arrived, I think all the flora and very nearly all the fauna were peculiar to New Zealand, but since then the competition of exotic species is driving a lot of the native New Zealand species to the wall.

The general impression left by the people is of a very provincial community. Though this is the era of jet flight, and they are no farther from London than Edinburgh once was, they still feel much as they did when New Zealand was some months away by sailing-ship. It is a grand country for the small dairy farmer – a reasonable degree of affluence, a nice climate and plenty of facilities for outdoor sports. For anyone with more cultural or intellectual ambitions it is indeed a desert, and all the more gifted young people are anxious to get away, preferably to England or North America, but they would settle for Australia rather than stay where they are.

The last time I was in New Zealand I flew to Christchurch in the South Island and strolled out of the hotel into the cathedral to fill in time before supper. I was surprised to see the arms of my Oxford college in the porch, and it was thus I learnt that the town is called after the college, because it was founded largely by graduates of the House. I had been a member of the college for forty-five years and had never heard on any single occasion of this connection between the college and the principal city of the South Island.

I think it is generally understood in Australia and increasingly so in New Zealand that for defence they must look to the United States, and for trade to the Pacific area. Though circumstances have compelled this reorientation about which neither we nor they can do anything, there is an extraordinarily strong sentimental bond between these countries and the United Kingdom. It is this bond which we should foster far more than we do. The most poignant experience in travelling round is to see the long list of names on the village memorials of Anzacs killed in the two wars – particularly in the First. Though they were fighting in part for themselves, they were fighting mainly for us.

North America

My first visit to North America was on my honeymoon in 1923. We went on a cargo boat from Purfleet to Botwood in Newfoundland and back with a cargo of paper in reels. The voyage out was uneventful but we sailed back through a raging Atlantic gale with sixty foot waves. Fortunately we had a full cargo and a following wind, so it was possible to enjoy the beauty of the scene. Newfoundland at that time was a miserably poor country and an independent Dominion. I seem to remember that it claimed to be the oldest Dominion. Its politics were very corrupt, and I can recall the indignation expressed over the outgoing Premier Sir Richard Squires. It appeared that he enriched himself from public funds to the tune of £250,000. This was quite acceptable in itself but he had cleaned the Treasury completely out.

We visited a logging camp on a Sunday and found the men singing hymns, but what impressed me most was the scene in the kitchen. The cook had taken out his false teeth and was imprinting a scalloped pattern round the edge of the Sunday tarts. Conditions were pretty rough. The choppers slept on wooden shelves softened by bunches of heather-like stuff called cutter-brush, a great contrast to the logging camps of today with wonderful meals, comfortable beds, washing machines, drying-rooms and buses to work.

My next visit to North America was in 1937 when I went to Canada in connection with the affairs of the Anglo-Canadian Company in Quebec City. My most vivid recollection of that trip was a flight down the north shore in a seaplane to visit the Gulf Pulp Company at Clarke City, about three hundred miles down the St Lawrence. We arrived all right, but trying to take off on the return trip the plane struck a sandbank, and we stood out on the floats until a passing Indian saw our plight and got help. I was rather relieved at the idea of going back to Quebec by boat, as I had no confidence in our pilot who seemed even more nervous than I was myself. However, having proceeded about one hundred miles towards Quebec in the boat I was disappointed to see our seaplane lying at anchor awaiting me. We took off successfully this time, and set a course straight for Quebec over thickly forested country. We had a head wind and were flying low. The pilot said it was about three hundred feet. Suddenly our only engine failed and we dived for the tree-tops. I gripped the arms of my seat and thought, 'This is the end'. However, before we actually hit the trees the engine picked up and away we went. In all, the engine failed three times, and towards the end the petrol gauge registered no petrol. I asked the pilot what we were flying on: evidently not petrol. He said 'My reputation!' However, we landed safely at Quebec, and the engine finally failed as we taxied in. It was many years before I ventured up in an aeroplane again.

In my memory I may be telescoping two trips to Canada and the United States. But anyway in 1937 or 1939 I expressed a wish to see the Middle West. So I was told Iowa was a typical mid-western state, and as I was to be in Chicago in any case I would drive to Des Moines, the only town of any importance in Iowa. The principal papers in the state were owned by a retired banker called Cowles and run by his two sons, and it was on this trip that I met Mike Cowles, who had just launched the magazine *Look*. It is now one of the great magazines of the world, showing nothing of its rustic origin in Des Moines. Mike Cowles and his brother have the principal newspapers in Iowa and Minnesota as well as *Look* and other minor properties. The brothers may not have been quite so successful as Henry

185

Luce, but Mike has the advantage of being the nicest of the major publishing tycoons of the world.

Also before the Second War I met Captain Paterson, who had founded the *New York Daily News* with great success about the year 1919. He was no charmer but a ruthless, though very able editor and publisher. He and his eccentric cousin Bertie McCormick had made the *Chicago Tribune* an immense commercial success. Later there was obviously no room for two men of such pronounced personality in the same enterprise and they decided on Northcliffe's advice to break into New York with a paper like the *Daily Mirror*, so that Paterson could run the New York paper while McCormick had the Chicago one. It was said that these cousins in establishing the supremacy of the *Tribune* had played some part in the rise of Chicago gangsterism. Anyway, they were accused by their competitors of burning rival newspaper vans, breaking the arms of boys delivering competing newspapers and so on. He has been depicted by his family and his firm as a simple Christ-like figure. This is rather typical of American business which in practice is as hard-boiled as it is possible to be, but they love putting up notices of the principles on which their particular business is run, usually a string of platitudes, admirable in themselves but not noticeably applicable to the business concerned. Both McCormick and Paterson were descended from Medill, who founded the *Chicago Tribune* and played a large part in founding the Republican Party. So you would have thought the family would have rejoiced at any sign of budding talent in the younger generation. But not at all. Alicia Paterson, Captain Paterson's daughter, was never allowed to play any serious part in the *Daily News*, and so went off and founded her own paper *Newsday* in Long Island. This has been a fantastically successful venture, reaching a sale of 400,000 and making excellent profits for herself and her Guggenheim husband. Alicia herself, alas, died fairly young, perhaps the ablest and most successful of all women newspaper founders and publishers.

I paid no visit to North America until 1945, when Bart wanted me to go to North and South America to see about syndicating rights in *Mirror* material. It was possible to get a permit on the grounds of a visit to San Francisco to report the founding of the United Nations, in which I was not interested, as I did not anticipate for it any greater success than the League of Nations had enjoyed. This is how I found myself on a troopship in the Clyde, filled mainly with Canadian soldiers' wives, women they had married while stationed in England and who were journeying to Canada for the first time. These British wives were a sorry lot and included some prostitutes. Within a few hours of their reaching the boat the Canadian Commander had to issue a warning that if the behaviour of some of them did not improve they would not be allowed to enter Canada. There were also a number of journalists on their way to San Francisco. I shared what was originally a two-berth cabin with Claud Cockburn, Iverach McDonald of *The Times* and Philip Jordan of the *News Chronicle*. McDonald was very serious: Claud Cockburn was not, but Philip Jordan was the life and soul of the party, making me roar with laughter at seven a.m., a feat which I should have thought impossible. He had a wonderful story about going over the Yildiz Kiosk in Constantinople immediately after it had been occupied by Allied forces in 1918. What struck him most was a glass chute down which concubines reached the Sultan's quarters.

The voyage was long and rough: we were twice attacked unsuccessfully by submarines and arrived safely, after about twelve days, in Halifax. The dramatic moment of the trip was one night when the convoy was blacked out and we heard of the death of Roosevelt. The anti-dramatic moment of that journey was VE day in a hotel in Miami. There was some small local election on, so all the bars were closed. No interest of any kind was shown in Churchill's speech: in fact the event was almost wholly ignored.

Since then I have paid so many visits to North America that my experiences have become merged. But to begin with Canada.

In the course of years I have seen most of Newfoundland, Quebec, Ontario and British Columbia and parts of Labrador, Nova Scotia, New Brunswick and Manitoba. What always amuses me is talk of the 'emerging nationhood of Canada' and poppycock of that kind. Canada is not a country: it is the northern fringe of the United States. It looks huge on the map, but when you get there you find that the country is five thousand miles long and only two hundred miles wide. The rest is uninhabited desert. The relationship is not between one part of Canada and another but between Canada and the part of the United States immediately to the south. Reeds have a paper mill at Dryden in Western Ontario, but when the staff go shopping in the big city, they don't go to Toronto, still less to Montreal, but to Minneapolis. Mr Bennett, the Premier of British Columbia, is far more concerned with his relations with the State of Washington than his relations with Ottawa, which he regards as a distant and hostile power. Newfoundland to him might well be on another planet.

We have heard a lot about the Separatist movement in Quebec and I must say I am not surprised. Since 1937 I have been concerned with the affairs of the Anglo-Canadian Pulp and Paper Mills. The mill is perhaps the largest enterprise in the city of Quebec, which is about ninety per cent French-speaking, and it gets its pulp wood from areas which are one hundred per cent French-speaking. Yet all the good jobs used to be held by English Canadians. Laval University in Quebec was concerned to train priests, lawyers and doctors and until recently had no facilities for teaching engineering or forestry. This provided an excuse for giving not only the engineering jobs but most others to English Canadians. I think at the mill only one per cent of the departmental heads used to be French-speaking. We held the controlling interest yet any effort to change this by us was consistently obstructed, and there is a limit to the steps you can take to alter the attitude of some Canadians to other Canadians. This determination to treat the French Canadians as second-class citizens was only altered when the present agitation began, particularly when it was reported, falsely as it turned out, that the Separatists had put a bomb in the Company's mill. Certainly now as far as the Anglo-Canadian business is concerned the situation is in a fair way to be rectified, but an awful lot of time and goodwill has been wasted.

Of the Canadian politicians I have met, the one who impressed me most was M. Duplessis, for many years the Premier – almost dictator – of the Province of Quebec. He was himself a man of financial integrity but unfortunately the same could not be said of all his supporters. He had great political and considerable administrative ability, had immense personal charm and spoke faultless English. He could even make very funny jokes in English, the final test of bilingualism. On the next level down I would put Joey Smallwood, Premier of Newfoundland, and William Bennett, Premier of British Columbia. Smallwood is a fiery little man who, over a long period of years, has done a great deal for Newfoundland. Bennett, with more stature and less dynamism, has done a tremendous amount for British Columbia. These three men are or were round pegs in round holes. The Prime Ministers at Ottawa have had an impossible job. Mackenzie King, whom I never met, seems to have been an arch-trimmer. R. B. Bennett, whom I did meet, was far too forceful to last long in Federal politics. Lester Pearson was a brilliant civil servant, an acceptable Foreign Minister but a disastrous Prime Minister. He had little political sense and presented a weak and flabby image to his public. John Diefenbaker rather put me off by saying 'Call me John' the moment we were introduced. This is supposed to be friendly, but surely the principal object should be to maintain the dignity of his office, not to impress me with his friendliness. He had an evangelistic quality in his politics but was a poor administrator.

When you enter the United States from Canada you pass from the provinces to the Metropolitan territory. Canadians always seem to me to be Americans without the courage of their convictions, living high on American investments in the natural resources of their country. The United States is so huge that it is impossible in a lifetime to know it well, but I can fairly say I have visited at different times most areas, the West Coast, the mid-West, Texas, the deep South and the Atlantic seaboard from Washington to Boston, as well as Miami.

The newspapers are poor things, with the exception of the *Wall Street Journal* and the *Washington Post*. The talent that used to go into American newspapers at a time when they led the world now goes into magazines and into television. Much of the television is very poor because of the huge volume of material used, but the best is as good as any. The present news-paper proprietors are not very outstanding. Jack Knight has had much commercial success with his papers, notably with the *Miami Herald* which is not particularly distinguished for its editorial content, but mechanically and commercially is prob-ably the best-equipped newspaper factory in the world. The man with the most newspapers is Sammy Newhouse, a charming little man you would never see in a crowd, yet he has built up a string of papers, many of them important and all more successful than Hearst's were in his hey-day. He also bought control of *Vogue* to please his wife. His newspapers belong to a trust which minimizes his tax liability. His rivals have always been envious of the very large amounts of capital he seems to have at his disposal. Like Roy Thomson he is only interested in the commercial side of his newspapers: their political stance does not interest him.

The Sulzbergers who own the *New York Times* are the nicest people, but little has happened to enhance the reputation of the paper since the death of the late and great Adolph Ochs. It is now a dropsical production in which everything seems sacrificed to volume of advertising. There is excellent material buried be-tween the advertisements, but it is spoilt by verbosity, repetition and the sheer difficulty of separating the little wheat from the vast amounts of chaff.

The United States is a commercial and industrial power, and

the commercial and business capital is New York. It is only fairly recently that Washington has ceased looking like a larger Canberra or Ottawa and has begun to look its part as the political and administrative capital of a world power. Even so, it is New York which is the exciting city. Seeing New York for the first time is an experience no one forgets. If any city is pure twentieth century, this is it. It is a wonderful place to be rich in, but quite appalling to be poor in. I have often been through the slums of Harlem, formerly on foot, but now it would be too dangerous. I have been through the worst streets in Detroit and Chicago and seen housing conditions that would not be tolerated in some much poorer countries. I suppose there is some lingering remnants of the old Nonconformist idea that wealth was evidence of God's favour, while poverty was proof of the reverse. Thus the poor have not only the deprivations of their poverty but the contempt of their more prosperous fellow-citizens. To look at it another way: in England in the last century and in the United States to a great extent today, the race is to the swift and the battle to the strong: the weak, the ill, the ignorant, the lazy and the stupid are just trampled under foot. In this country the pendulum has swung the other way and a solicitous State takes far more trouble over the feckless and the delinquent than over the brilliant and the diligent.

American manners are quite different from ours. Traditional English manners have been to keep new acquaintances at a distance until you have decided you want to know them better. The American attitude may have begun with lonely people lost in a vast empty continent. On meeting new acquaintances you greet them by their Christian names, which you keep on repeating. You want them to feel liked, or preferably loved. A world empire has long since cured us of any hope of being loved, and Americans will eventually have the same experience.

As the years go by, American culture is bound to diverge more and more from ours for all sorts of reasons, but in particular because of our quite different attitudes to women and to death. These are quite fundamental, and in time are bound

191

to set the two countries on courses which will take us further and further apart. In England the man is the head of the family. We all know numerous exceptions to this, but the rule generally holds throughout Europe and still more in Asia and Africa. In the United States the mother is the boss, though of course anyone would know many exceptions to this too. All sorts of theories have been advanced to account for this fact and my guess is no better than anyone else's. Of course some of the jokes about the all-American female are grossly unfair, but there is a residue of solid and important fact.

In this country death is treated unemotionally as a disposal problem. Half our dead are cremated – much the highest cremation rate in the world – and funerals are cheap and matter of fact. In the United States funerals are expensive: embalming is universal for those who can afford it: dead soldiers have to be flown back from the battlefield. Death is big business. At this point I cannot resist putting in two funny stories. The most interesting sight in Los Angeles is the cemetery at Forest Lawn. It is an excellent site beautifully maintained, and contains three mortuary chapels of which one 'The wee Kirk i' the Heather' is a popular venue for smart weddings. Last time I was in Los Angeles I thought I must have a look at this little church from the inside. I was startled to see that the stained glass windows were devoted to the story of Annie Laurie! Good provision was made for weddings, including rooms for the bride and for the bridegroom in one transept. Balancing these rooms on the other side of the church were some large cupboards. I asked what they were for: I was told they masked the crematorium ovens!

When in New Orleans I asked to see over a Funeral Home, that great American contribution to the art of gracious living. This was thought a trifle eccentric – why not look at our lovely suburban homes, including that of Dorothy Dix, the original giver of newspaper advice to the love-lorn? The advertisement manager of the *Times Picayune*, one Murray, who took me to the funeral home told me he hadn't been there since the death of his stepmother. As they carried her down the stairs, with the coffin open, as is the custom, he noticed what white feet she had. So when he got back to his office ready to make his daily bet, he was interested to see that one of the runners was 'Pale Toes'. So he put a larger sum than usual on 'Pale Toes' which won at long odds – 'and that was all the good my stepmother ever did for me!'

I regard my annual visit to the United States as a battery-charging operation. Certainly in industrial matters the Americans have courage and they think big. It is a great contrast to the frustrations and delays in this country to see their huge projects forging ahead. Their management of large corporations is mostly good, and far better than ours. Their preoccupation with money, and only money, is excessive, and their so-called religious activities are pretty nauseating. Their church-going, which is almost obligatory, seems purely social with no discernible spiritual content. But for all that, their sins are sins of commission for the most part. Americans are active and positive, and certainly when I got to Washington I was always relieved that the maintenance of peace as far as the western world is concerned rests on the American leaders and not on our own much smaller men in Whitehall.

In 1952 I found myself crossing to America on the same boat as Lord Beaverbrook, who asked me to dinner in his suite very soon after our arrival. The only other guest was Ben Smith, the Wolf of Wall Street. He had made a large fortune on the bear tack in the great slump of the early thirties, and had put up much of the money with which Garfield Weston had invaded the biscuit and bread-making industry of this country. Ben Smith was a power in the Democratic Party in New York City and strongly urged us to vote in the Presidential Election next day! He could easily arrange for us to vote, impersonating some deceased New Yorker, and wouldn't it impress our friends when we got home to say we had voted for the American President? Reflecting on the enormous fuss there would be if we were photographed emerging from a polling booth, we both declined.

I didn't meet Eisenhower or any of his Administration. What could one say if one did? But the Kennedy Administration was quite different, and when I had met some of his closest collaborators, I met some of the other major figures around. The ablest of them all was Macnamara. His history in office showed he was a poor politician, but as an administrator he was superlative. Within my time we have never had a Minister of remotely comparable ability. American business tycoons – and Macnamara had been President of Fords – are often able but usually predominantly tough. This is not true of Macnamara. For all his ability he is a very nice man. I had two long talks with him, in one of which he gave me a detailed account of the confrontation over Cuba, and I was immensely and most favourably impressed.

If you want a complete contrast to Macnamara, there is Dirksen, the Republican leader in the Senate, where he is one of the members for Illinois. From the English point of view he is a figure straight out of the last century, yet a majority of his constituents must be citizens of Chicago. He has a deep voice and unruly hair, and to parallel his appearance in this country one would have to go back to family albums of provincial figures of the eighties or nineties. His politics and political methods would seem to have no connection with the twentieth century, yet in his own country and his own State he is a real power in the land. The politician I liked best was Hubert Humphrey, charming, amusing, liberal, a most attractive man. In English politics one could see him going straight to the top. In the 1964 Presidential Election it was he who said, 'Behind every successful man stands an astonished mother-in-law.' He is the son of a poor chemist in Minnesota and has come up the hard way. His image may have suffered during his years as Johnson's Vice-President, but he is a good man and a nice man who made a very considerable mark as a Senator.

The Senate is a curious body, as it seems to have usurped the power surely intended by the Founding Fathers for the Lower House. I once asked a Senator if his position among his fellow-Senators depended on the State he came from, so that the Senators from New York or California would be of greater weight than those from Vermont or Nevada whose constituents are mostly trees and cacti respectively. Apparently not. A Senator's standing depends on his seniority and personality. I remarked to one Senator that I had met a Senator from a New England State who seemed a paragon of stupidity. He said indeed I was quite right, but Senators never publicly attacked each other for stupidity, womanizing or drunkenness. I suppose those in glass houses are wiser not to throw stones. Perhaps this is why John Kennedy, a compulsive womanizer, was criticized for everything else but his principal fault.

I have met President Nixon twice, not alone; I think he has had an unduly bad press over here. There has been a great deal of controversy over the question of Nixon's polilical integrity and he is certainly not a great man, but he is highly intelligent, immensely hard-working, exceedingly well-informed, a professional politician to his finger-tips and he leaves our Ministers looking like fumbling schoolboys. I don't think he would go over well as a politician in this country, but that is irrelevant. He is an American politician, not a British one. The same applies even more to President Johnson. He is inconceivable as a leading figure in British politics, which makes it harder for us to judge him than President Kennedy who, with some adjustments, would have dominated English politics.

I had a long talk with Johnson after he had been President for some years. He is a big man but not a great man: a superb Washington politician but not a good national one. When I was with him he gave me two impressions, that he was out of his depth on Vietnam but obsessed with it, and that he could not keep it out of his conversation that he was doing his utmost to be a good President, but found his quite appalling past very difficult to shake free from. Of course he said nothing to this effect, but while watching him I had a very strong feeling that this was so.

Of course not all the Washington figures are giants. There is

195

Harriman who is a rich man, full stop, or Rusk who is a dull man, full stop, or Henry Fowler, no comment. But in the second rank there are, or were, McGeorge Bundy with quite the quickest, clearest brain of anyone I ever met, and so nice with it all; George Ball, who was the second man at the State Department and who would be a great Secretary; Vance the Deputy-Secretary for Defence, when I met him, who would be an adequate Prime Minister in most countries; Helmes, the head of the CIA, a most intelligent, capable man and so on and so on.

Perhaps at this stage, having described several men as 'nice' I should say what I mean by this description. Briefly, I think people are nice if they put more into life than they take out of it.

Of the younger men, I was most impressed by Lindsay whom I met first when he was one of the Representatives for Manhattan. He is a most attractive man, at that stage anxious to get into national politics, but wondering how. The Governorship of New York State and the two Senatorships were held by men who were likely to be there for some time, so his only hope, a forlorn one so it seemed, was to have a try at being Mayor of New York City. As a Republican he would have a poor chance to win in an overwhelmingly Democrat city. However, nothing venture, nothing win. He became Mayor, and a good one, and we are likely to hear more of him in the years to come. Another up-and-coming member of the Lower House is Mr Bolling from Kansas City, a most engaging type. He is likely to end as Speaker of the House and one of the major figures in Washington. I met a very impressive Representative from Fort Worth who had hoped to have a crack at one of the Senatorial seats for Texas, but failed to raise the funds necessary for the campaign which, particularly in a large State like Texas, ran into many hundreds of thousands of dollars.

Of recent years the most interesting personalities have been the Kennedy brothers. For anyone to want the Presidency as much as John Kennedy did is a sign of immaturity. To regard that office as a prize to be won, a trophy to be carried off, is to take a very shallow view. The responsibilities of the office are so immense that no man can hope to be more than inadequate. When Truman was told Roosevelt had died and he was President, he was said to have told the reporters who broke the news to him 'Pray for me boys. I feel as if the sun, moon and stars had fallen on me.' Surely this is the right attitude. But once in office Kennedy gathered round him the ablest men he could find and grew to realize what it was he had undertaken. I had forty-five minutes with him in a few weeks before his assassination and thought he had the makings of real greatness. It is curious how squalid the surroundings of the President are. To avoid the Press, one is ushered in through the basement. The waiting-room is like a sitting-room in an inferior country hotel. When moving from the waiting-room to the President's very fine oval office (with bullet-proof windows), one sees young men in the passage stand up. I was assured this was not out of respect for me, but because they could pull their revolvers quicker when standing up than when sitting down. When I was received by President Johnson it was in a tiny little room not more than ten feet square and heavily curtained. One reads about all these very necessary precautions but when one sees them they really are most disturbing. I saw President Johnson arrive at the White House with General Ne Win, the President of Burma. The car was surrounded with guards of all kinds with two plain-clothes members of the President's special police standing on the rear bumper facing to the rear. After the carefree way our Royalties and Ministers drive about, it is a great contrast. A difference doubtless is that the rulers of America and Russia are worth assassinating, but this country and its rulers are no longer that important.

I had an interview with Bobby Kennedy when he was Attorney-General, a much more important office in the United States than it is here. The American Attorney-General is a sort of Minister of Justice. Bobby Kennedy was obviously a man of great ability and immense energy but to me not impressive –

too much of a little man in a hurry. I thought Teddy Kennedy more likely to go far. Like his brother the President he is strikingly handsome. As a very young Senator he is in no hurry. He does not seem to have the ability of his two brothers, but he has the name and is perhaps a nicer man than the President and much nicer than Bobby. To be fair, those who saw a lot of Bobby after Jack's death say he was a much improved character, and that he had sloughed off a lot of the go-getting brashness that so grated on me.

I have twice made speeches in Washington, once to the Press Club and the second time to the annual conference of the Newspaper Editors. On both occasions, separated in time by several years, I expatiated on the poor quality of the contemporary American newspapers. This was very fully reported, but what was not reported at all was my belief that American politics are hopelessly out of date, and that this is dangerous not only to American citizens but to us all, now that the United States is one of the only two world powers. In America they have been toying with Medicare, but in Europe the Welfare State had been inaugurated by Bismarck in the 1880s and by the Emperor Franz Josef in Austria in the 1890s, and no one could say they were exponents of 'creeping socialism'! In most advanced countries it has been accepted for decades that the State should be responsible for a minimum level of medical care and of education of those who cannot afford it. In America this is a live political issue, and even now if you are a poor negro in one of the poorer states of the Deep South your chances of a good education or of proper medical care in your old age are minimal. These are only examples of the state of politics in the United States. When Americans lead the world in technology of all kinds, why do they allow their politics to remain in the 'horse and buggy' stage?

Europe

There have been various plans for a closer relationship between ourselves and the French, one in 1940 and others between the different European countries after the War. In common with most Englishmen I didn't pay much attention to these suggestions, which I took to be little more than pipe dreams. My business connections took me mostly to Canada, West Africa, the United States and Australia, though in the ordinary course I had met Adenauer, that solid block of granite, when he was Chancellor of Germany and Mendès-France when he was Foreign Minister of France.

However, I was dining one night in Ghana with the Jacksons when Lady Jackson (Barbara Ward) said she had just returned from a conference in New Zealand and had come to the conclusion not only that joining the Common Market was the best policy for this country, but that opposition from the Commonwealth would be far weaker than had been supposed. I have known Barbara for thirty years and regard her as perhaps the greatest living Englishwoman. So I pay great attention to anything she has to say. On the Common Market she entirely convinced me that the future of Britain lay with Europe, not as an independent off-shore island, or as an American aircraft-carrier anchored off the coast of France. It was following this talk that I swung our newspapers in support of the movement to get us into the Common Market. After the *Mirror* had embarked on this policy, the other newspapers joined in and eventually the London newspapers were all in favour of our joining the Common Market except for the *Express* group. Though this campaign went on for a long time and though it was known that the Prime Minister, Harold Macmillan, was also a Common Market man, the Government made no sign. Eventually I went to see him to ask him, if he was in favour of the Common Market, why didn't he say so? He had almost the whole Press on his side. What was he waiting for? Though I had an hour with him and asked this question three times in different words, I got no reply, nor did I ever hear what inhibiting factor was at work. When he did come out with his bid to join the Common Market it was an effort so half-hearted and so late that it deserved to fail. It was said that the approach was not more enthusiastic for fear of stiffening the terms for admission. But surely it was the Prime Minister's business to think of his own people first. This would represent an entirely new direction for our foreign policy, and one that should have been put over with conviction to the people of this country. Moreover, to have done so would have convinced the peoples of the Continent that this was a serious change of policy and of heart, and not just a manœuvre.

To me the Common Market policy is not just the best for this country: it is the only policy. For four hundred years the whole world has been our oyster, but now that the different countries of our former Empire are independent, and that modern communications have reduced the size of our planet, we must form part of a larger unit, and both geography and history have dictated to us that that unit must be at least Western Europe and in time, we hope, Eastern Europe as well. In a Common Market moving towards a united Europe, we have much to give and also much to receive. It provides us with an objective and a policy. Without this policy we are limited to parochial interests and narrow horizons.

Once having decided that our future lay with a Europe trying to unite, I tried to use such resources as were at my disposal to further this policy. First I went to meet Jean Monnet, the creator of the Common Market, the greatest European of them all, and in spite of this I found him so modest and so charming. He has an optimism that is sometimes misplaced, but a faith which has already moved mountains.

In the course of the negotiations Ted Heath did a superlative job, though perhaps it would have been wiser to join the Common Market first and negotiate afterwards. I seem to remember that at one time they were negotiating over the tariff on polo sticks, and certainly the negotiations got involved in so much detail that one rather lost sight of the wood for the trees.

The *Mirror* had for long had an office in Paris, before the War with *Paris-Soir* and afterwards with *France-Soir*. The pre-war proprietor of *Paris-Soir* was Jean Prouvost, a woollen manufacturer from Roubaix or thereabouts. He was deprived of his newspaper after the War, but he started up again in the publishing business and established the highly successful *Paris-Match* and *Marie-Claire* as well as owning a majority holding in *Figaro*. He is now at eighty one of the liveliest of the important newspaper publishers of the world. His editor before the war was Paul Lazareff who started the paper *France-Soir* for Hachette after the War and repeated the success he had had previously with *Paris-Soir*. He had not quite the same degree of success because, following on the German occupation and the division of France into Occupied and Unoccupied Zones, the French provincial newspapers have greatly strengthened their position, and are now collectively much more important than the Paris Press. So *France-Soir* has not more than half the sale of its pre-War equivalent. Paul Lazareff's wife is one of the more fascinating elements in French journalism, and in addition to her very great personal charm is the very successful editor of *Elle*.

It was in the Lazareffs' house that I met Couve de Murville and Pompidou. I thought from his appearance and from the fact that he had been managing director of the Rothschild banking firm that the latter was a Jew. But not so, he comes from the Auverone or thereabouts and is therefore a fellow-countryman of the notorious Laval. I suppose one would assess both Couve de Murville and Pompidou as civil servants of the highest class – Pompidou perhaps something more, at any rate recently, which may be why he was so summarily retired.

From our side of the Channel the régime of de Gaulle looks high-minded and austere, if sometimes wrong-headed. A few hours in Paris with the journalists stationed there and one is told one hair-raising story after another of corruption in high places. No one accuses de Gaulle himself of corruption, but his close associates include some people who do not live up to his example. The Ben Barka case came as no surprise to the Paris-based journalists. Because de Gaulle is an imposing personality people suppose he must be a great statesman, but imposing personalities need be no more than imposing person-alities. It would seem to me that his great service to France was to restore to Frenchmen their self-respect. He has been a dis-aster for Europe, and his ideas of making France a world power are merely expensive illusions. His hostility to England and the United States is based on his experiences during the War when he felt he was being treated with less than appropriate defer-ence. We should of course have either backed him or ditched him. We didn't do either, to our – or France's – great detriment. I have only seen him once, in the War in the Savoy Hotel, when I noted at the time that he looked very much like a king in exile.

In 1966 there seemed to be almost no official relations between the British Government and the French, so why not at any rate establish contacts between the principal editors of the two countries? So we invited thirty leading proprietors and editors to London as our guests for a few days to meet an equivalent number of English editors. The French editors were mostly strongly anti-de Gaulle but the two things that struck us most as hosts was that they seemed to have no more idea than we had on what the General was likely to do next. The other source of surprise was that these leading French newspaper people in a surprising number of cases had never met each other, and a number of them, particularly of their wives, had never been to England. As I regard Hugh Cudlipp as the best popular newspaper editor of his day, so I regard M. Beuve-Méry, editor of *Le Monde*, as the outstanding editor of a serious paper. The essential difference between the two kinds of newspaper is that the popular paper is bought mainly for entertainment but partly for news: the serious newspaper is bought for information and opinion though it may contain an element of entertainment such as a crossword puzzle.

My social relations with France and the French began in 1920 when it was thought desirable that I should learn French, and through mutual friends I went to stay with a Comte d'Orléans at their château at Rère in the Sologne about halfway between Blois and Bourges. It is pine and heather country, rather like Scotland only flat. The d'Orléans are not related to the French royal family but are aristocrats of the finest vintage. They have occupied their present property for six hundred years and are one of only half a dozen French families of which this can be said. The Count was very unlike our idea of a Frenchman, a rather silent man with grey eyes and a very quiet dignified manner. His wife came from the south, a daughter of the Marquis de Château Renard, who was at one time Ambassador in St Petersburg and later in London. They had three children, Alberic the present Count, Charles my friend and Jacqueline, now a Marquise. To these people the Revolution was still current history. Titles given by Napoleon were thought nothing of, and families that had bought property belonging to *émigrés* in the 1790s were people one would not care to know or to intermarry with. Charles was always engaged in discussing with his mother a suitable bride for himself. In these matrimonial calculations there were three elements, birth, money and health, so that a penniless duke's daughter threatened with tuberculosis was the equivalent of the rich healthy daughter of a pork butcher. Madame d'Orléans was very realistic, and apt to laugh at her son when his aspirations went beyond his standing in the marriage market. In the end Charles made what was

considered a suitable match, and after the wedding fell violently in love with his wife, and was inconsolable when she died
in child-birth. When he married again he was so upset he wept
throughout the ceremony.

With Charles I went to various dances, one a ball in the great
château at Blois. The girls were stationed with their mothers
round the edge of the ball-room. They had to be returned to
mother at the end of the dance. For the bolder spirits there was
usually a room for sitting out, called a 'flirt-room' but there
was very little flirting. Girls were very strictly chaperoned,
though it was almost permissible to tip a little brandy unnoticed
into your partner's champagne, hoping that this would render
her slightly more affectionate. I could not play tennis with
Jacqueline alone, though the court was in full view of the whole
house, without one of her brothers standing by – this in spite
of the fact that I was a hopelessly shy and awkward youth and
she was some years older than I was. When in my turn I took
Charles to a Caledonian Ball in London, I thought it was a
very pretty sight with men in kilts and the girls in long white
frocks with tartan sashes. Charles's comment was 'Very
undecent'.

Immediately after the War I rushed over to Paris to bring
Charles coffee and soap and other things I knew to be in short
supply. But the door of their home was opened by his widow.
He had taken part in the Resistance and had been shot in the
leg. His wife had carried him on her back through the streets of
Paris to a place of safety. But he was arrested again and died of
diphtheria in Mauthausen camp.

I have never had any close contacts with Germany – after all,
in the thirties we were always denouncing Hitler, and then there
was the War and the post-War period when Germany seemed
utterly ruined and smashed. My interest really only surfaced
when Axel Springer appeared on the scene. He is the son of a
small printer in Altona, a suburb of Hamburg. He had missed
military service owing to ill-health, and at the end of the War
was equipped with one typewriter, and his office was an air-

raid bunker. His first paper was *Hör Zu*, a sort of *Radio Times*. This was a huge success, and with the proceeds he launched *Bild Zeitung*, now enjoying by far the largest sale ever reached by any German newspaper, about four million. He modelled it on the *Daily Mirror*, and so there have always been close links between his organization and the *Mirror* office. We are not particularly proud of this stepchild. It practises all the cruder arts of the sensational tabloid press but has neither warmth nor compassion. For it to become a great paper Springer must surely learn to love his readers. Since then he has bought *Die Welt*, one of the three serious papers in Germany, and has established a number of magazines. He has become vastly rich but much criticized, even hated. This is not in any way personal. He is handsome, charming and cultured, but he has little political ability and his public relations have at times been deplorable. He controls a very large proportion of the entire German output of magazines and newspapers and this gives him great potential power, but to make the power actual he must stick to the interests of his readers and to objectives that are attainable. His politics have been erratically right wing, and his main interest has been the reunification of Germany, which he has seen as realizable in the near future. Some years ago, in Berlin, he assured me that Germany would be re-united in ten months! To his credit he has been very pro-Israel, but he has been very unsympathetic to the aspirations of German students and other young people. Moreover, he has not realized sufficiently that with such an immense publishing empire he must be exceedingly careful of his public image, if he is not to have his empire taken from him.

Axel Springer entirely dominates the popular press of Germany, but his paper *Die Welt* is probably not profitable. The outstanding serious German newspaper is the *Frankfurter Allgemeine Zeitung*, produced by half a dozen very lively minds. I should imagine it will grow in circulation and authority. It is the successor, in a sense, of the pre-war *Frankfurter Zeitung*, a highly respected journal. It is an advantage, too, to be published in Frankfurt, which should obviously be the capital of Western Germany, and would have been had not Herr Adenauer been born in Bonn.

When I was in Germany in 1967 I met some of the leading German politicians. Herr Kiesinger is so like Harold Macmillan it isn't true. He could easily be Macmillan's younger brother with some of his mannerisms. He had a difficult coalition to lead, but the general German opinion seems to be that he is weak and ineffectual. He has been blamed unfairly for doing nothing to help us into the Common Market. His explanation to me was that his immediate preoccupation was the improvement of Germany's relationship with Eastern Europe, which is why the Roumanian Foreign Minister was in Bonn at the time. In this endeavour the French could be helpful, so (he implied) why choose this moment to quarrel with them over Great Britain? I think this policy probably sound. The reunification of Germany, which must be the primary objective of any German Government, is only to be realized by some degree of reunification of Eastern and Western Europe, and better relations between Western Germany and her Eastern neighbours are a sound move in this direction.

On the same visit I had breakfast with Herr Strauss, formerly Minister of Defence, but then and now Finance Minister. He speaks excellent English and is a lively and immensely able man. I have no doubt we shall be hearing much more of Strauss. Politically he more or less controls Bavaria, and with the declining importance of Ruhr coal, the industrial centre of gravity in Germany is moving south, towards Bavaria. On top of all this, Strauss is the best mob orator in German politics. Of course, however strong he becomes with the Catholics and the South, there is always Schiller, Economics Minister, the Protestants and the North.

The Social Democrats do not seem to be so well endowed with political talent. Willy Brandt, who did a magnificent job as Mayor of Berlin, is a spent force, and Herr Schmidt, the leader of the Social Democrats in the Bundestag, is very able but has no *charisma*, to use the current phraseology. The most powerful figure outside politics is Dr Abs, the chairman of the Deutsche Bank. He is a very lively, immensely intelligent and capable man who has played a large part in the spectacular rise of post-War Germany, but his age makes it unlikely that he can be a force in the future. Though we tend to look with envy at the Germans' immense economic strength, that is not how it looks to Germans. They feel that politically the country is drifting, and neither of the big parties commands the loyalty or even interest of the younger generation. As an objective the re-unification of Germany is all very well, but that is a long way off and can only take place as a part of other changes in the relationship between the different European powers, and how is that to be brought about? Nobody knows.

I have always reserved Italy for my old age, though over the years I have been to Milan, Naples and Palermo and twice to Rome. The only newspaper worth talking about is the *Corriere della Sera*. In spite of its name, which means 'Evening News', it is a morning paper, and another paper with a different title is published in the evening from the same plant. The prize for the oddest title for any newspaper must be between *The Epitaph* published in Tombstone, Arizona and *Resto de Carlino*, the principal paper in Bologna, a title meaning 'change from a Carlino'. The title comes from the coin, as 'gazette' was once an Italian coin, not a publication (and scarlet a fabric not a colour). To return to the *Corriere*, it is a good local newspaper for Milan and the centre of North Italy. The other newspapers look like relics of the last century and are purely local. I have been engaged at different times in talks with Italian publishers over the possibility of the *Mirror*'s helping in the production of a national Italian newspaper. There are all sorts of difficulties of which the distribution problems are the most difficult. Italian publishers are much more interested in what is to go into the paper than in how the paper is to be conveyed to the reader, and this is often the nub of the matter.

Italian governments come and go but dominating figures seem

to be lacking. I have met Moro when he was Prime Minister and Nenni once or twice, a most attractive personality, but the real power has usually been wielded by the Vatican, and more recently the essential government of the country has been in the hands of Carli, the chairman of the Central Bank. It was he who got Italy out of its last recession. He is an exceedingly able, charming and cultured man, one of the real rulers of Europe.

When I was in Rome last I met a number of public figures and also one of the Monsignori at the Vatican to tell me how things looked from that observation post. This was interesting, and he threw in a story which I thought very funny. An old priest reproached a young priest for taking too much interest in a pretty girl who was passing by. The young priest protested that just because he was fasting was no reason why he could not inspect the menu.

Italian politics tend to be unstable, balanced as they are between the Vatican on one side and a very powerful Communist Party on the other. It is also hard for us to realize the difference of character of the different regions. We look at a map of Italy and tend to equate the country with England, which has been united for one thousand years, while Italy for barely a century. Moreover, the history of the different parts is so widely different. Sicily has been under foreign domination, Arab, Norman and Spanish, for so much of its history, while Venice, without natural frontiers, was independent for one thousand years before the Conquest of Napoleon.

Before coming to Italy I had supposed the Communist areas were those of the poverty-stricken deep South. But not so. These tend to vote Monarchist. The Red belt is around Bologna, a region of prosperous farmers and growing industry. The Communist influence here is because it was formerly part of the Patrimony of St Peter, the States of the Church, which were so abominably misgoverned for so many centuries that there is still a tradition of hostility to any government.

As part of our campaign to join the Common Market, the *Daily Mirror* published features about typical families in

France, Germany, Italy and Holland. The Italian family we chose lived in Naples. Our Italian butler who came from Venice was furious. He did not regard Neapolitans as Italians – hardly as human beings!

While our relations with Western Europe are of great importance, the problem of better relations with Russia and the rest of Eastern Europe is the problem that overshadows all others. There is little enough any individual can do, but that is no reason why we should not all do our puny best. Though I have been on friendly terms with the present Russian Ambassador and his two predecessors and have been to Russia three times, once in 1932 and twice more recently, one finds the Russians very baffling people. It has been said that the English temperament has been evolved partly by our climate and partly by our history as a trading nation. We seek compromise. The Russian character has been formed by the Russian winter. You win or you lose: you can't compromise. However that may be, Englishmen find Russians extraordinarily hard to understand. Perhaps it would be easier to establish friendly relations with the Poles or the Czechs, who were part of Western Europe until 1945, but are Slavs, and so might be a sort of half-way house between ourselves and the Russians. With this in mind, my wife and I established the warmest and most friendly relations with the Rodzinskis. He was the Polish Ambassador before the present one. He and his wife both speak perfect English and he is not a diplomat by profession, but a Chinese historian and scholar. Through him we were invited to visit Poland and spent a very happy fortnight visiting Warsaw, Cracow and other centres of interest. We subsequently toured Poland with the National Youth Orchestra. The most successful paper is the *Express Wieczorny*, edited by Mr Bielsky, the outstanding Polish journalist of the day. Their problem is that they are too successful, and their sale is greatly in excess of the official Communist paper *Tribuna Ludu*. This has to be checked from time to time by a limitation of the newsprint ration for the *Express*. In conversation with the chairman of the Press Trust I mentioned the poor state of the printing plant at the *Express* and said the International Publishing Corporation had a nearly new magazine printing press it could not sell and was proposing to scrap. It had cost £800,000 and they could have it if they would take it away. This proposition was the result of our acquisition of the Odhams Group, which left us with this surplus machinery at Fleetway. We could not sell it abroad – there were no buyers – and to sell it in the UK would have been to subsidize competition. The Poles were a bit incredulous at first but warmed to the idea, and eventually installed part of the machinery in Warsaw and part in Katowice. They explained they couldn't pay for this machinery but they had plenty of zlotys, and would transfer an appropriate sum to the municipality of Warsaw for the construction of a Musical High School – a musical high school because they knew of my wife's National Youth Orchestra. They suggested calling it after me, but I said surely a much better idea would be to call it after their great composer Chopin. This was the right suggestion as they had had a Chopin High School but it had been totally destroyed in the last War. Subsequently I laid the foundation stone and my wife performed the opening ceremony and I was given the Gold Badge for services to the City of Warsaw.

The Poles are charming people, much easier to understand than the Russians. But even a short stay in Poland brings home the terror of Germany in Eastern Europe. We tend to think that German military might was smashed at the battle of Stalingrad and that, awkward as the Germans often are in many ways, they cannot except in conjunction with the Russians ever again be a military menace. But this rather detached view is not shared by the Czechs or the Poles, to whom the horrors of the 1939–45 War are very present in their minds. And the Russians tend to harp on their common experiences in the War as a means of maintaining their grip on their Eastern European satellites.

To follow up this episode the *Daily Mirror* invited Polish journalists to London for a conference. There are really not enough editors for this, so we proposed to add Czech editors.

Then they said if two eastern countries were to be represented, why not two western countries, so we added some Dutch editors. Most of these various editors had never met each other, which is in itself a good thing. It also gave us an opportunity of meeting the Czechs, whom we did not know, and in particular Mr Svestka, the editor-in-chief of *Rude Pravo*, which is not only the official Communist paper in Czechoslovakia but outstandingly their best newspaper, with a sale far in excess of that of any other official Communist newspaper in any country having regard to the size of the population it serves. Mr Svestka, a huge bear of a man, was not only the dominating figure in Czech journalism and a very charming character, but a major force in the politics of Czechoslovakia.

This conference led to an official visit in 1967 to Czechoslovakia and Roumania when my wife and I met a number of the leading figures in both countries. They are all police states in the last resort, but in Poland and Czechoslovakia the individual can say what he likes provided his words are not published, and provided that no action follows, or at any rate that was the form last year. In Roumania, Government policy is far freer from Russian dictation than in the other satellite countries, but the degree of censorship and repression within the country was much more severe. We were there during the Israeli war, and it was quite impossible to tell from the Roumanian papers what was happening. I had an hour with Mr Novotny in Prague and with Mr Ceausescu in Bucharest. Novotny was at that time boss of the Communist Party and President, while Mr Ceausescu was Party boss but held no political office. At the same time there was no doubt in anyone's mind about who ruled Roumania. Novotny had been in a German concentration camp, and though more Stalinist than his successors, did not give the impression of a tough inflexible character as so many of the Russians do. He pointed out that he was receiving me in the same room to which the English emissaries had come to bully the Czech government into surrendering the Sudetenland in 1938. Mr Ceausescu is a livelier type, but that is perhaps due to the fact that the Roumanians are more Latin, and the Czechs are Slavs who have been under German rule for a long time. The result is a heavier, more serious national temperament.

But of all European countries Russia is by far the most important, and it can never be too late to start retrieving the many blunders on both sides over the past fifty years. The antics of the British Communist Party are no help in this regard. The Russia the tourist meets, or met until very recently, is friendly but incompetent beyond description. After overcoming the initial difficulty that Slavs do not answer letters or telegrams, you find yourself in a country where clotted incompetence at all levels reduces the visitor to a state of utter exasperation. At the same time obviously the Russians can be exceedingly competent when they want to be, as was seen in the War and in their achievements in outer space. They seem more confident in handling delegations than individuals, as when we went there with the National Youth Orchestra the arrangements worked without a hitch. The audiences were marvellous and the trip was a great success. One odd incident sticks in my memory. The orchestra arrived in Kiev for a concert, prepared to play the national anthem of the USSR. The Kieff authorities would have none of this and demanded the Ukrainian national anthem. We had never heard of such a thing and the orchestra could not of course play it, so we had no national anthems, British, Russian or Ukrainian! This nationalist feeling was evidently very strong, as even the boats in the river were all flying the Ukrainian flag.

But difficult or no, the Russians are one of the two superpowers, and it is up to all of us to come to a better understanding with them. It would be a help if they were not so suspicious and more ready to help their friends to be friendly.

Religion

I was brought up a member of the Anglican church. In Ireland the church is very 'low', in every possible way the opposite of the Irish Catholic Church which is particularly reactionary. I was what is called a 'black Protestant'. At that time, of course, religion had a very strong political tinge. If your name was Kelly you were a Catholic and a Home Ruler: if your name was Pakenham you were a Protestant and a member of the ascendancy.

My parents were regular church-goers, but I don't think they had any very definite beliefs. At school in England the Protestantism was not anti-Catholic, but I cannot say I met anyone who really believed anything. The Church of England has always seemed to me to be like Barclays Bank, an honest and honourable institution, doubtless containing among its members many individuals of profound religious convictions, but not in itself a religious organization. I was brought up in a very anti-Catholic community, and I have always been antipathetic to the politics of the Catholic Church. But it seems to me that the Catholics, particularly in their religious orders, retain a sense of what religion is all about. This has been largely lost sight of in the modern world, so that to many people of today religion means either church-going, or morality, or just plain humbug.

One of my difficulties throughout life is an inability to take anything on trust. I have to work everything out for myself, so that with religion I could not start out with everyone else; I had to begin at the beginning. This was, I suppose, at my

213

Confirmation, when I told my house-master, a clergyman, that I found it impossible to believe in a personal God. This was brushed aside as a little temporary difficulty, which of course it is not. Confirmation got me nowhere, and I suppose it was at Oxford that I began to be interested. My father-in-law, Dr Cooke, was no great scholar and an ineffective head of a family, but he was sincerely and deeply religious and had a spiritual gift. I was lonely and read a great deal, as I had always done, and I suppose it was about that time that I read the *Cloud of Unknowing*, the greatest mystical book written in English, dating from the fifteenth century. Over the years I have read other books of the same date and kind, notably the *Scale of Perfection*, and from that I have gone on to the books of the greater writers on mystical religion, Christian and other. Of these I make most of St Theresa of Avila, but find St John of the Cross beyond me. There is greater understanding of the mystical world in India, but Hindu and Moslem authors write in such an unfamiliar tradition that all you can say is that their experiences are similar. And they all seem to find difficulty in fitting in their experiences with the particular religious group to which they belong. They have a direct apprehension of God, and find that this experience has no relationship with the Thirty-nine Articles of the Anglican Church or their equivalent in other churches. They also find it impossible to give a coherent account of their ecstasy, but all are agreed that it is the most important of all human experiences.

If you take these people seriously, and I do, then religion is not a matter of dogma or of observances, but of establishing a relationship with God. Evidently to many people authority, theology, and such matters are all-important: to me they are insurmountable obstacles. Prayer to me can only be of value if I am alone. But many people, presumably most, find praying in a congregation much easier.

Of course, all this had to be learnt, and it takes time, as I had no-one to help or to teach me. To me the Virgin Birth and so much else is incredible history and unhelpful myth. The value of the Bible is in the teaching, not in the history or in the dogma. I cannot accept the doctrine of the Redemption, and I don't see that it matters anyway. We are given in this world an opportunity to contribute to God's purpose. It will be attained anyway, but perhaps it is in the power of individuals to hasten or delay the attainment by some infinitesimal amount. There are people whom I respect who *know* that there is an after-life. I have never myself thought it likely and have no inner conviction on the subject. The idea of my personality surviving into the remote future in however spiritualized a form seems to me unattractive and improbable. There must be some form of immortality, not necessarily personal, as some churches, particularly those surviving from the Middle Ages, have an almost tangible atmosphere of devotion. Modern churches, on the other hand, have no more atmosphere than a branch of Barclays Bank.

It has seemed to me that while mystics in all countries and at all times have claimed a direct apprehension of God, there are other devout people with more limited spiritual gifts who have an appreciation of part of God's nature or purpose. In this connection I was interested that Sir George Thomson, the Nobel prizewinner, once told me that great scientific discoveries are made by men who *know* what will be the significant experiment to make. If such a man plodded away at the experiments which might be significant, he would be most unlikely to turn up anything interesting in a life-time. Once, of course, the big leap forward has been made, there will be other lesser men to follow up and fill in the gaps.

It seems to me that these great scientists must have a direct apprehension of a part of creation, and to this extent are in the same sort of category as the great artists of the world. The difference surely between a great artist and a gifted technician is that the former has a spiritual quality, some channel of communication with God, that the latter lacks. And the Divine is orderly so that great art is a revelation of the Divine Order, while so much of modern art in all disciplines is merely a reflection of the disorder of the world in which we live. At the present time there is no great art, because for the time being the world is not interested in beauty but in nature. Hence the prophets of the present are the scientists, and twentieth-century revelations are scientific. That doesn't mean that they are not revelations of the Divine – all truth is of God – but that that is the kind of revelation we are seeking. Have we not been told, 'Seek, and ye shall find'?

If, of course, you are seeking to discover God's purpose, you are necessarily conscious of living your life in His presence. Every standard of behaviour, however high, once attained is seen to be inadequate. However successfully you purge yourself of sins of commission you merely become the more aware of your sins of omission, and as everyone always could do more and could do better, sins of omission will always remain with you.

It seems to me that this approach to life provides the logical basis for morality, because it is soon seen that sin cuts you off from the Divine presence. You also learn that the most serious sins are not those of which we hear most, murder, theft, adultery and so on, but envy, hatred and malice. The former sins depend for their seriousness on circumstances, while the latter are unconditionally sins.

Of course if you are always aware of the presence of the Almighty, vanity should be impossible: any achievement seems utterly trivial compared with the sweep and scope of the whole of Creation. On the other hand, such awareness gives an authority and a confidence which cannot be gained to the same degree in any other way.

People have told me at various times that I have some spiritual gift, but this does not seem to me to be so. I can sometimes discern in others a spiritual gift of which they themselves are often unaware. But even this discernment is very uncertain. When I went to India in 1946, it was mainly to meet Gandhi and see if he had any answer to the problems of religion today. I asked him specifically if Hinduism could contribute anything to the spiritual famine of the West. He said no. I gathered that Hinduism was too old and now too corrupt to be of any help. The point I am trying to make is that on his record Gandhi had a huge spiritual gift if anyone in the modern world has had one. But I could not pick it up. I am not arguing that therefore he had no spiritual gift but that my antennae could not receive on his wavelength. This is such a non-religious age that people who know they have some special relationship with the Almighty tend to keep very quiet about it for fear of having it destroyed. Many others are unaware of any such gift and put any influence down to 'charm'.

The British are not a religious people, but an intuitive people, and this has been the essential basis of our greatness, not that it has been in evidence these last twenty-five years. This intuition may have a spiritual basis. I believe that this quality remains alive in our people, though not in our leaders, and it is to this that we must look for any regeneration.

Two new factors of religious significance have emerged in the last century. The first is the time scale. It used to be thought that the world was created about 6,000 years ago: it is now known that this took place about 4,000 million years ago. The universe was created earlier, at least 10,000 million years ago, and if the 'steady-state' model proves correct may have been in existence always. This to me makes a huge difference, because if the world were only 6,000 years old you could reasonably expect significant changes for the better in your own life-time. It is now clear that human beings have existed on the earth for at least a million years, so that there is plenty of time. God is not mocked. It follows further that the remote purposes of God are unknowable. We seem to have descended from very primitive creatures, perhaps plants. It would have been as impossible for those creatures to have foreseen the human being as it is for us to see the future in millions of years' time. All we can hope to see is His purpose for us now.

We now know more about the scope of the universe not only in time, but in space. So scientists are now familiar with distances much smaller than a millionth of a millimetre, and such vast spaces are known in astronomy that they are meaningless to ordinary minds. And in time there are not only significant periods that are immensely long but others that seem to us inconceivably short. For some particles a millionth of a second is a long life-time. Thus the scope of the creation is far wider than our ancestors had any means of knowing. For the ancient Greeks, one of the most intelligent communities that ever lived, events that took place forty years before a man's birth were in a period obscured by the mists of antiquity.

The other discovery that has religious implications is that it now appears that all life on this planet had a common origin. There may have been two creations of life, but more probably one, so that all animals and all plants have a common origin with ourselves. Saints in the past have felt this to be true, but it is important that there is now irrefutable scientific evidence that this indeed is so.

There is understanding through knowledge and understanding through love. When I was young I thought I might attain some measure of salvation through knowledge, as my knowledge is very extensive. I found that this was not so; and later I learnt that in the old controversy on whether Salvation was to be gained through Faith or through Works, the answer is Faith not Works, though in most cases faithful people are not purely contemplative.

What our society lacks is love for each other and for all living things. Spectacular successes have been achieved by a society run too much on envy and greed. Happiness eludes us and wisdom is rare. It is perhaps in this sphere that we may learn from some more primitive societies. Our immigrants are horrified at the way we treat our old people, and I can remember my father telling me that Indians were appalled to learn that we actually had to have a Society for the Prevention of Cruelty to Children.

Various religions in the past have depicted this world as the battlefield on which the forces of good and the forces of evil contend; though good will win in the end, the battle sways to and fro meanwhile. I don't myself believe this doctrine, but if it were true we have seen in my life-time evil winning every skirmish, not by the achievements of any monsters of iniquity, but by the qualities of the Laodiceans who blew 'neither hot nor cold'. We call it the permissive society in which all good traditions crumble. A crash would bring about a reaction, which would be much more healthy. Of course there are a few positively actively evil people about, but very few compared with earlier centuries. On the other hand, there are far fewer people with saintly qualities. Mediocrity is everywhere.

It has been argued that success in business is only to be achieved by dishonest means, or at any rate without any great regard for integrity. I should have thought the commercial success of the Quakers is sufficient proof that this is not so. In my own career I have been interested to find that success is to be had even with the maintenance of high standards of integrity. It is this and the satisfaction of running a successful organization that, with the beneficent exercise of power, have been the satisfactions my working life has brought me. Money has not meant much to me, partly because my enormously rich uncles were obviously unhappy and partly because the pursuit of personal wealth is an inhibiting factor in any religious advance.

I think some people are born with spiritual gifts not given to others. Was this the original significance of those who were recognized as the 'elect'? These gifts can be lost with misuse or enhanced by cultivation. Those born without them can only acquire a lesser degree of spiritual awareness. The most conspicuous case of loss of great spiritual qualities in our own day has been Hitler. It would seem that much misuse can be redeemed with repentance, but there comes a point of no return, and then your Hitlers and Napoleons find themselves reduced to the level of ordinary men. The final loss of power in both men seems to have occurred at the time of their invasions of Russia. I have often wondered if the Russians, a profoundly religious people, are under some special protection as the Jews of the Old Testament believed themselves to be.

219

Recent student disturbances in America and France have been led by middle-class students, sometimes to the horror of their working-class contemporaries. The reason is simple. In a materialistic society, such as ours, you promise your young people affluence if they work hard and really apply themselves. In this search for affluence a degree is a great advantage, so working-class students do not wish to damage their careers by rioting. But to offer affluence as a goal to middle-class students is meaningless, they have the affluence already. To offer a car in every garage, a chicken in every pot, as Hoover did, is all very well but not if you already have two or even three cars in the garage. So these students complain of the quality of life today. And surely what they mean is the lack of any spiritual quality in contemporary life. There is no attempted answer to the age-old question, 'What are we here for?'

One question which has caused more controversy in my life-time than any other has been that of sex and marriage. On this the teaching of Christianity has seemed to me to be ambiguous and materialist. The guilty feeling about sex which permeates Christianity does not extend to other religions. My father used to tell me that a devout Moslem says grace before going to bed with his wife, 'For what I am about to enjoy, may the Lord make me truly thankful' or words to that effect. In any case why deplore and decry sex, or teach that it only exists for the procreation of the species? This is a very narrow and rather sour view. In fact sex is not only the source of the most intense physical pleasure available to mankind, but under favourable conditions can be the source of great spiritual experience. The objection to promiscuity is that promiscuous people, particularly women, find they have left part of themselves with several or many men and can never reassemble themselves whole again. Before it became a joke, perhaps this was the original meaning of a 'ruined woman'. And of all the sins of society the worst seems to me to be prostitution. It may well be that it has existed in most, if not all societies, but this is no excuse. The idea of bartering sexual intercourse for money or money's worth seems to me horrifying. If anything is sacred in life, that should be it. And the ordinary reaction of blaming or despising the prostitute seems to me contemptible. The blame rests on the customers, on the demand not the supply, and the inducements offered by men to weak and often silly women are such that they cannot reasonably be blamed for succumbing.

The great religions are now very old, and expressed in terms appropriate to a very different society. Hinduism must be 3,000 years old: Buddha and Lao-Tze lived about 2,500 years ago: Christianity is 2,000 years old and Mohammedanism 1,300 years. So surely it is not unreasonable to hope for a religious revival in the not-too-distant future. Presumably when the time is ripe a great religious teacher will declare himself. Much needs to be done by way of restating the eternal truths of religion in terms comprehensible to dwellers in the vast cities of the future, and great religious teachers of the past have always carried the world forward a step as well.

Colophon

Do you remember the Theban, somewhere in Herodotus, who says – that of all human troubles the most hateful is to feel that you have the capacity for power and yet you have no field to exercise it. That was for years my case, and no one who has not been through it can know the chilly paralysing deadening depression of hope deferred and energy wasted and vitality run to seed. I sometimes think it is the most tragic thing in life.

Herbert Asquith to Mrs Horner, 1892

Index